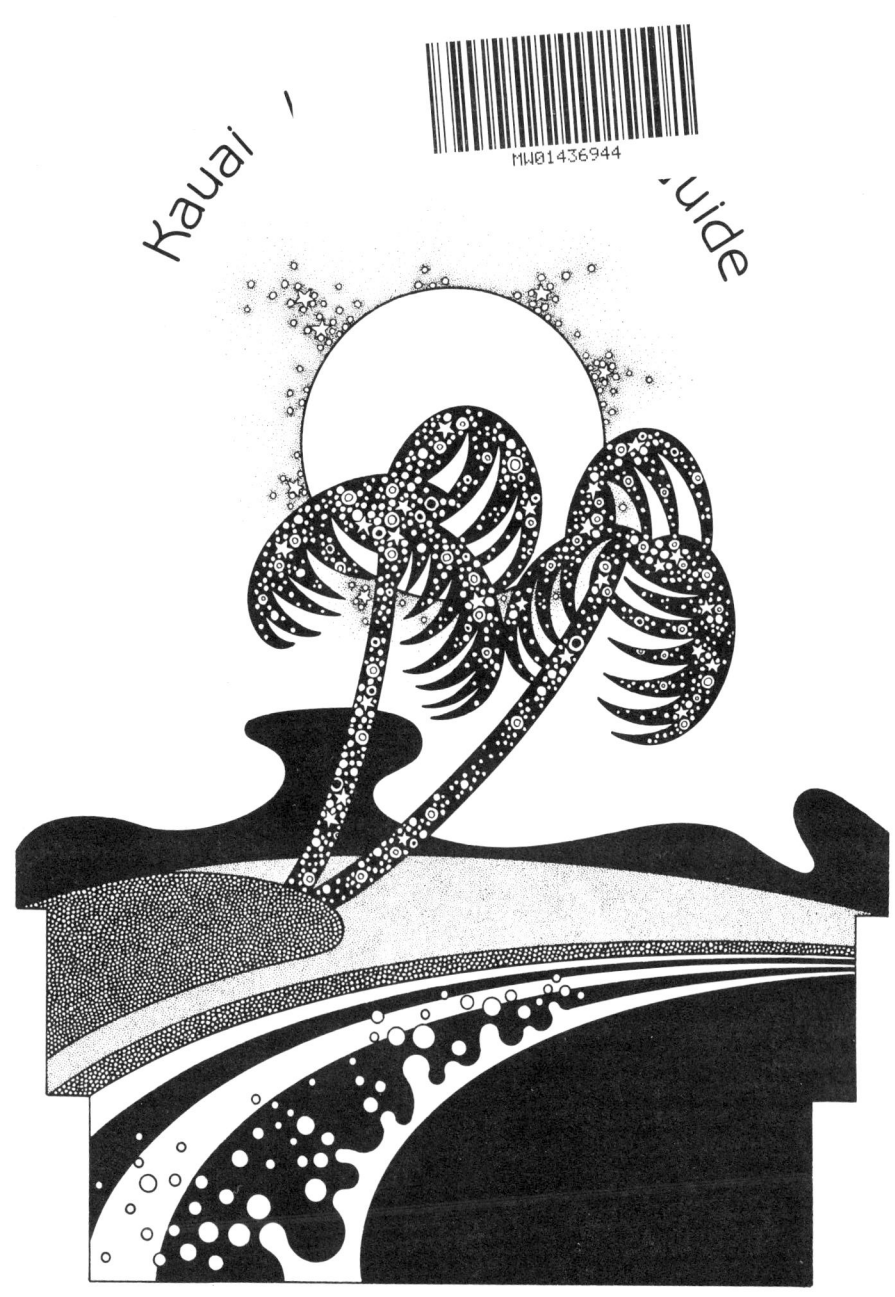

Lenore W. Horowitz

©1992 by Papaloa Press, a Division of LCH Enterprises Inc.

First edition:	1980
Second edition:	1981
Third Edition:	1982
Fourth edition:	1983
Fifth edition:	1984
Sixth edition:	1985
Seventh edition:	1986
Eighth edition:	1987
Ninth edition:	1988
Tenth edition:	1989
Eleventh edition:	1990
Twelfth edition:	September, 1992

All rights reserved
under International and Pan-American
copyright conventions.

ISBN 0-9615498-5-8
ISSN 1045-1358
Library of Congress Catalog card 82-643643

Technical Assistance by Kate Meyer Design, Palo Alto, CA
Printed in U.S.A. by Griffin Printing, Sacramento, CA

Contents

Beach Adventures

North Shore, 13
Eastern Shore, 28
South Shore, 35
Westside, 39

Restaurants

North Shore, 49
Eastern Shore, 70
South Shore, 124
Westside, 146

Exploring Kauai

Touring Kauai, 11
Sunset Drive to Hanalei, 62
Helicoptering Kauai, 154
Boat Tours, 158
Museums and Special Tours, 162
Hiking & Camping, 165
Riding & Running, 168
Hawaiian Entertainment, 169
Golf, 168
Island Tastes, 170
Kauai Specialties, 173
Flower Leis, 174
Shopping, 175
Children's Corner, 179
Special Mornings with Daddy, 181
Travel Tips, 183
Traffic Hints, 186
  Restaurant Index, 188
  Index, 190

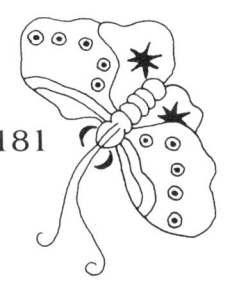

*Special thanks to Lauren, Michael, Jeremy, Mirah,
and Larry Horowitz
for their invaluable help
with the research, writing,
illustrating, and designing of this
twelfth edition.*

Preface – Magic Kauai

When we wrote our first edition, more than a dozen years ago, Kauai was the undiscovered island. Resorts were relatively small-scale and low-rise, for development was strictly controlled, and buildings could be "no higher than a coconut tree." A tourist could walk for miles on spectacular beaches and encounter only another person or two. Two of the island's three traffic lights were in the main town of Lihue, and the third was at a sugar cane road intersection near Koloa, a sleepy town where the Salvation Army building had the freshest coat of paint. Most of the island was inaccessible, and the main road stopped at either side of the island's northwest quadrant — the spectacular Na Pali wilderness reachable only by boat, helicopter, or narrow and dangerous hiking paths.

Today, most of this is still true, though now more than a million visitors discover Kauai each year! Tourism has grown to more than three-fourths of the island's economy, and hotel rooms number over 7,000. Three new luxury resorts have catapulted Kauai into jet-set vacationing, with an airport runway extension under construction to accommodate the wide-body jumbos. A dozen traffic lights are needed to control traffic, and in spite of a new by-pass road near the airport, Kauai can still have mainland-style bumper to bumper traffic jams along the main two-lane road at rush hour. Everywhere, people talk about traffic, and even at some of the prettiest beaches, you may be listening to the roar of the helicopter tours as much as the crash of the surf.

You can still find the magic Kauai, though, if you make the effort to look. So far, development has affected only 4 % of the island, primarily in the south near Poipu and in the east near Lihue, with the rest of the island zoned for conservation or agriculture. Once you drive north of Kapa'a, or west of Hanapepe, you turn the clock back ten years. Mile after mile of pastureland and cane fields stretch to the sea, for the rainfall in the north and the barrenness of the west have so far provided natural barriers to development. While you will find more to do and eat and see than ever before, you can still find beautiful places to be alone.

This is the Kauai we will try to describe to you in our *Guide*— not what you would see from a tour bus, but the rare and special place we have discovered over the years as tourists and homeowners. We want to share with you our favorite adventures—at the beaches, in restaurants, and on shopping expeditions. We do not describe every restaurant and shop, only those we have visited, and our opinions are shaped by personal preference. We look for peace and quiet, privacy and natural beauty.

In many ways our *Guide* is unique. As a family of six, we can offer advice on beaches and activities based on having taken children to Kauai for more than fifteen years! For adults with that enviable freedom to go off by themselves, we describe in detail what one can expect to find in many island restaurants. Even a single year brings dramatic change to this island, and our working vacations keep us busy tracking what's new, what's different, and what's still as lovely as ever. You may find that in some cases prices, policies, even managements may be changed, so do your research carefully when making decisions and keep us posted about what you find out. It's been great fun hearing from people all over the country who have enjoyed discovering Kauai with our *Guide,* and who want to help update the next one.

So as we go to press with our twelfth edition, we want to thank all the readers who have helped make our *Guide* a storybook success. Who would have thought that our first edition of sixteen pages would grow into a book which has sold more than 70,000 copies! Or that our oldest child, Mirah, would arrange such a spectacular send-off by handing our first edition to a friend she made on the beach. He turned out to be Chandler Forman of the *Chicago Sun-Times*, and when his story about Kauai—and our book—was syndicated nationwide, more than 700 letters arrived at our door, and we had to rush to press with a new edition!

When she arranged this PR spectacular, Mirah was a gregarious six-year-old with two baby brothers. Today, our youngest child, Lauren, is nine, and Mirah at seventeen flies to Kauai by herself, fitting our family vacation into her own agenda. Our boys are changing too, their love for sandcrabs and rainbow shells giving way to a passion for surf. When they were small, we hoped one day to escape from all their clutter. Today, toy cars and crayons are off the floor at last, but now Jeremy and Michael each bring friends, and each of the friends is bigger! We seem to be spending quite a bit of time at the airport picking up arriving friends or sending suntanned friends back home. Rather than offering advice about traveling with young children, we should perhaps offer tips at arranging independent travel for teenagers!

Watching our children change so dramatically over a dozen years helps put the development of Kauai in perspective. With children and with islands, change brings the excitement of new opportunities and at the same time the loss of what was precious. The roads we drive today are certainly more congested, but our destinations are also far more interesting. Once perfect for our family with small children, Kauai is also perfect for a family with teenagers, with definite and sometimes contradictory interests. And as we explore their newest horizons, we see this wonderful island unfold in fascinating new possibilities.

Like an old friend, Kauai gets better with each visit. New adventures take us to new places, and at the same time we rediscover with deeper affection what we have loved in the past. We hope you will feel the same way about this special place and return again soon!

Beach Adventures

North Shore, 13
Eastern Shore, 28
South Shore, 35
Westside, 39
Map, 16 & 17

Notes

Touring Kauai

Kauai is like an America in miniature, with rolling hills and valleys to the east and majestic mountains to the west. On the eastern shore, sand as fine as sugar rings half-moon bays fringed with stately ironwood trees. These are the best beaches for walking and hunting for shells and driftwood. On the south shore, the island's flat, leeward side offers protected swimming almost all year round under sunny skies and gentle breezes. We love the north shore, where magnificent cliffs reach to touch the sky, and the foaming, churning surf crashes against the rocks. Here, rain showers freshen the air, dance among the flowers, and make the coastline sparkle. Or go west to Polihale Beach, where you'll find cliffs like the exotic towers of some lost civilization, and golden sand stretching as far as the eye can see. Kauai will never bore you, because a half–hour drive, at the most, can take you to a beach that almost seems to belong to another island.

Different as they are, the beaches also change their moods with the seasons. In summer, the sea may be so calm and clear that bubbles on the surface cast shadows on the sandy bottom. But winter tides can turn a peaceful lagoon to a roaring, raging caldron; and ocean spray will drape the valleys with salty mist. In winter, some north shore beaches disappear entirely under crashing surf, and boats which anchor peacefully in Hanalei Bay for half the year take shelter in Nawiliwili to the south. Even the sunsets change with the shifting angle of the sun. In winter months, when the sun rides lower in the sky, you'll see the sunset in burnished clouds over the mountains, while in summer, the slender line between sea and sky catches fire in a torrent of gold.

Almost circular in shape, Kauai has three main tourist areas. If you plan carefully, even a short visit can show you a little of everything. Kauai is nearly encircled by a main two-lane highway, except for the wilderness area in the northwest quadrant. This main road is easily traveled; you can get from Lihue to Kapa'a in about 20 minutes, from Kapa'a to Hanalei in about 45 minutes, or from Lihue to Poipu in about 20 minutes, and from Poipu to Polihale in about 35 minutes.

Pack a picnic lunch and some beach mats, and explore the island's most beautiful hidden beaches! In our book, we have arranged the beach descriptions to follow the route you would travel if you were driving clockwise around the island, beginning at Ke'e Beach at the westernmost end of the road on the north shore, and then driving south along the eastern shore towards Lihue and then west towards Poipu, Kekaha, and finally Polihale, the magnificent beach at the end of the road on the westside.

We don't recommend that you follow that route! Instead, read about the beaches and plan your destinations according to the weather and the season. In winter, the surf is more unpredictable and dangerous on the beaches to the north and north-east, while the best and safest swimming is on the south shore. In summer, the surf may be up on the south and west, with north shore beaches beautiful for swimming. Whenever you head for the beach, however, follow this simple rule for swimming safety: don't swim alone or too far out at any beach whose currents are unfamiliar to you. Be sure to read 'Beach Safety' (page 44-5) carefully.

No matter the season, try to explore as much of this wonderful island as you can, especially the north shore where the beaches are by far the most spectacular. They're not as much fun in the rain, however, so plan your travels with an eye to the weather. On a clear day, drive north, because if your visit to Kauai is only a few days, you may not get another chance! If you see rain out your window, on the other hand, drive south to Poipu or west to Salt Pond or Kekaha, where the weather is usually drier. On a really rainy day, unless the storm is island-wide, Polihale might be your best—even your only—dry option! When in doubt, call 245-6001 for the weather and surf report.

North Shore Beach Adventures

Ke'e Beach

When you can drive no further on Rt 560 on Kauai's north shore, you will discover a beach so beautiful you won't quite believe it to be real. The Na Pali cliffs rise like dark green towers behind the golden sand, and a reef extending out from shore creates a peaceful lagoon ideal for summertime swimming. As you walk along the shining sand, new cliffs come into view until the horizon is filled with their astonishing shapes and you begin to imagine princesses held captive in enchanted castles.

Like all windward beaches on the north shore, the surf at Ke'e Beach varies with the seasons. Winter surf can reach 20 feet, and then the ocean roars with crashing waves and churning foam with undercurrents far too strong for safe swimming. In summer, however, the turquoise water can be perfectly still and so clear that bubbles on the surface cast shadows on the sandy bottom.

Snorkeling can be spectacular close to the reef, even in the shallow water where you can stand up at will, and the water, though warmed by the sun, will feel ice cold along the surface from rainwater. The coral reef is shallow enough to walk on, but you'll need sneakers to protect your feet from coral cuts. Be careful too of unpredictable currents in the channel to the left of the reef, as they can be strong enough to pull a swimmer out of this sheltered area into the open sea.

Large trees at the beach provide shade for babies and protection from the occasional rainshowers which cool the air and make the coastline sparkle. Small children can play and swim safely in the shallow water or climb over the rocks at low tide. Bring nets and pails for small fishermen! They will also love collecting limpet shells or the tops of spiral shells.

Because of an unusual combination of low tide and calm summer sea, we were able to walk west across the rocks and around the point for the first time in more than six years. From this vantage point, the Na Pali cliffs are truly magnificent—jutting into the cobalt blue ocean in vivid green ridges, the surf crashing in thundering sprays of foam. This walk is too dangerous to attempt in any but the calmest sea, and you must watch the direction of the tide carefully so that your return trip does not involve crossing slippery rocks through crashing waves. Ke'e Beach, lovely as it looks, can have treacherous currents and unpredictable surf, and so extra caution is a must. Showers and restrooms are available. If possible come early and come midweek, for parking at this lovely and popular spot is hard to come by, especially in summer.

Ha'ena Beach Park

An icy stream winds across this lovely golden sand beach curving along the coastline. The water is a dazzling blue. Reefs bordering both sides of the beach, named *Maniniholo* after the large schools of convict fish feeding on the coral, provide summertime snorkeling, when the waves are gentle enough for swimming and rafting. During winter months, however, large waves can break right onto the beach, making swimming, even standing, a hazardous activity! Restrooms, showers, picnic and barbecue facilities are available, as well as camping by permit. You might even find a sandwich truck if you forget to bring lunch! You can walk a long way in both directions, with spectacular views of the towering cliffs and shimmering sea.

Tunnels Beach

You'll see lessons in snorkeling and scuba diving at Tunnels Beach because this large, protected lagoon is so perfect for swimming. Tunnels is protected by two reefs, the outer reef favored by surfers for perfect arcs, and the inner reef filled with cavities and crevices to explore for fish and sea life. This is about the only beach on the north shore that is usually calm enough for beginners, although even here you may find rough surf and treacherous currents during winter months. Listen to the surf reports and plan any winter visits for times when surf is flat on the north shore, and preferably at low tide!!

In summertime, bring the kids and let them paddle about on boogie boards while the older ones try their luck with mask and snorkel. Bring a plastic baggy of bread crusts, release them one at a time and you'll be surrounded by fish! Swimming through the coral formations of the reef, which is almost like a maze of tunnels, can be great fun when the water is quiet. Enter the reef through one of the small sandy channels or the large one on the right, and hundreds of fish in rainbow colors will swim right up to your mask. If the showers which frequent the north shore rain on your parade, you can take shelter under the ironwood trees—or under your boogie board!

Tunnels can get crowded, particularly in summer. The beach is the departure point for Captain Zodiac boat tours, and both swimmers and the boats have to share the large sandy channel through the reef. The zodiac staff may try to motion you out of the channel to make way for the boats, but don't be intimidated! People—not boats—have the right of way. On the other hand, keep a lookout for the boats and be ready to get out of the way if you have to. You may see a seal lying on the beach. Give it a wide berth; it's probably exhausted, resting before heading back out to sea! Seals don't trust humans and need privacy to recuperate.

Even between May and August, when the area between the two reefs may look calm enough for safe swimming, watch out for these danger signs: high surf on the outer reef or fast moving ripples in the channel between the reefs. These indicate powerful, swift currents that could sweep you out through the channel into open ocean. At those times, hunt for shells on the beach instead of swimming, or walk around the rocks to the east, where you may find sunbathers with very dark tans in all the best places!

Directions: On Rt 560, drive 1.1 miles west of the entrance to Charo's at the Hanalei Colony Resort. You will pass the mile 8 marker and the turnoff to the YMCA camp. Parking is difficult if not occasionally impossible. The area close to the beach is fenced off. Just look for all the cars on the shoulder, get as close as you can, and walk in. No public facilities.

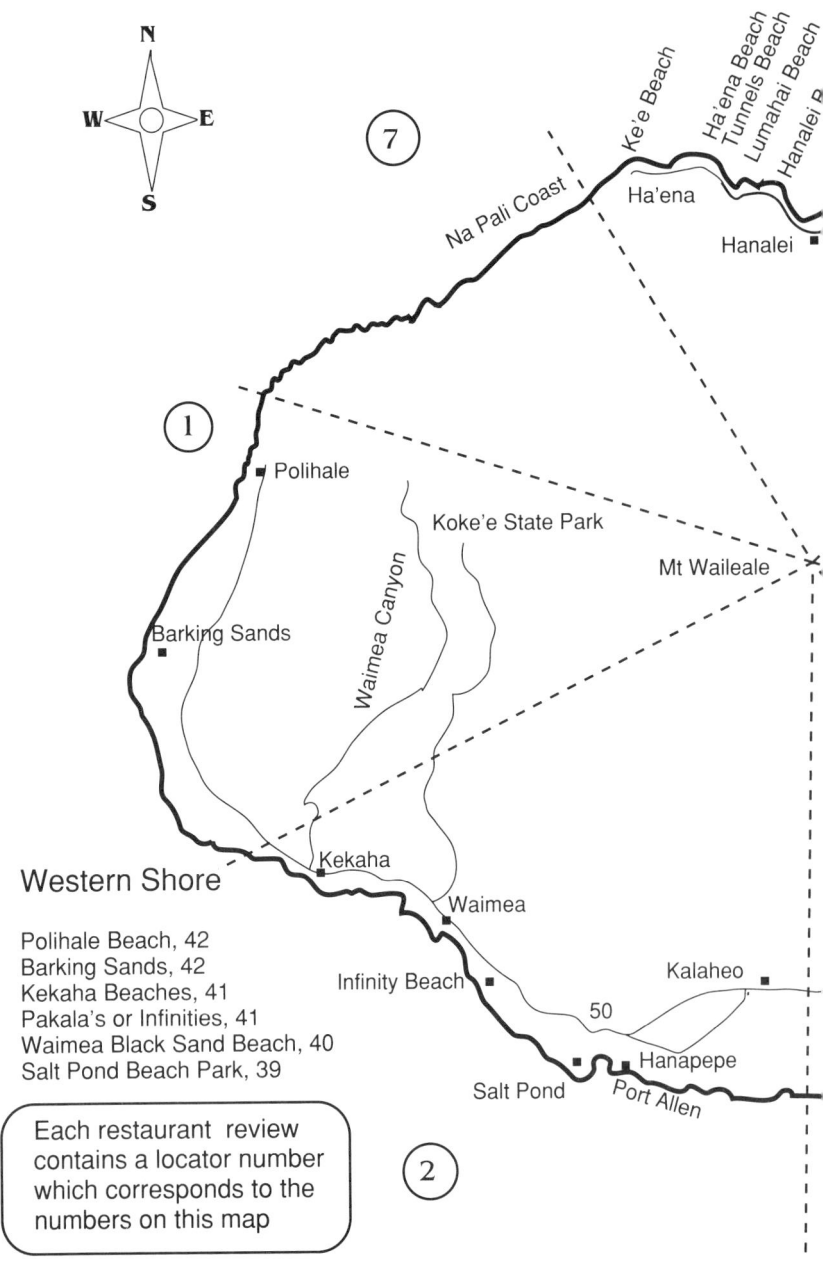

North Shore

Moloa'a Bay, 27
Larsen's Beach, 25
Kilauea Bay, 23
Secret Beach, 21
Kalihiwai Bay, 20
Sunset Beach, 20
Anini Beach, 19
Hanalei Bay, 18
Lumahai Beach, 18
Tunnels Beach, 14
Haena Beach Park, 14
Ke'e Beach, 13

Eastern Shore

Kalapaki Beach, 33
Ninini Beach, 34
Hanama'ulu Beach, 32
Lydgate Beach Park, 31
Kapa'a Beaches, 31
Kealia Beach, 30
Donkey Beach, 29
Anahola Bay, 28

South Shore

Poipu Beach Park, 37
Brennecke's Beach, 37
Shipwreck Beach, 36
Mahaulepu Beach, 35

Lumahai Beach

The setting for the Bali Hai scenes in the movie South Pacific, Lumahai Beach is stunningly beautiful, a curve of white sand nestled at the base of a dark lava cliff, with a giant lava rock jutting out of the turquoise sea just offshore. Getting there requires a trek down from the roadside through slippery mud (showers are frequent on the Hanalei side of the island), and the trip back up is even worse, especially if you have to carry a tired child. If there are toddlers in you family, you might consider hiring a babysitter or buying a postcard!

Swimming at Lumahai Beach is dangerous, particularly during winter. There is no reef to offer protection from the unpredictable currents and rip tides which make Lunahai Beach one of the most treacherous on the island. Beware also of climbing that spectacular offshore rock for a photograph, as a sudden powerful wave can easily knock you off!

At the western end of Lumahai, about a mile further, is a beach with some of the biggest breakers we found; a sign warns against swimming in winter because of high surf and strong currents. The stream which flows into the sea here is ice cold from mountain rainwater, a refreshing way to rinse off sand and salt. After the waves break and the form washes over the sandy spit at the stream's mouth, miniature waves form and roll across the shallows for children to enjoy in summer months. There is no shade near babies near the water, however.

The stream meets the ocean at a huge rocky bluff, a spectacular place to sit quietly and wtach the waves crash against the rocks, sending dazzling spray into the air. It is also a beautiful beach for walking, although the coarse sand is hard-going near the waterline, and you must cross a vast expanse of hot sand to get from the parking area to the sea. Bring sandals! You can hunt for striped scallop shells shining in the sun, or wander all the way to the rocky bluff that separates this part of Lumahai Beach from the part pictured in all the postcards. Trying to cross the rocks would be hazardous, however, even at low tide, due to the occasional "killer wave" which can come up suddenly out of nowhere and smash you into the rocks. A small cave etched into the base of the cliff with a floor of powder soft, cool sand is a perfect spot for daydreaming and wave-watching, preferably with someone special.

Directions: Drive north of Hanalei on Rt 560 and look for the mile 4 marker. You'll see a lot of cars parked on a shoulder just past a 25 m.p.h. speed zone sign. Park on the right, opposite a No Passing Zone sign, lock up, and begin the hike down. To get to the western end of Lumahai, drive to the mile 5 marker, look for an emergency telephone by the road, and turn into a sandy parking area under the trees and beside the stream.

Hanalei Bay

Famous for its spectacular beauty, Hanalei Bay is a long half-moon of sandy beach carved into the base of a sheer cliff on one side and narrowing into a rocky point on the other. Several Trans-Pacific Cup Races from California to Hawaii end in this natural harbor, and during summer months, gaily colored boats rock gently at anchor on the eastern side where the Hanalei stream flows into the bay. Near the marina is a small park with picnic facilities and restrooms. Turn right off Rt 560 onto Weke Road, then right onto Aku Road. The park pavilion will be on your left.

You don't really need the park, however, as you can park near the beach by following almost any road off Rt 560 towards the water. The biggest breakers crest near the center of the curving coastline, where you will most likely see surfers hunting the perfect ride, although during winter months the surf can become too dangerous. In fact, boats are moved out of the bay by mid-October, and by winter, twenty-foot waves are not uncommon. Keep that in mind as you consider a zodiac adventure!

At any time of year, Hanalei Bay is fantastic for frisbee, the wide sandy beach firm and level for hard running. If you get hungry from all this exercise, look for the green Tropical Taco truck usually parked near the Hanalei Dolphin Restaurant.

West of the little town of Hanalei, still a cluster of weather-beaten buildings and quaint churches, are several beautiful places, and you can explore almost any road turning off towards the water and discover a lovely spot. At the westernmost curve of the bay, you'll find a calm, protected beach where the water is relatively quiet even when most of the north shore is too rough for safe swimming. At these times, the number of cars alongside the road will show you where to park!

Anini Beach

At the edge of Anini Road, you will find miles of white sandy beach protected by a reef. At some places the beach road is so close to the water that you could almost jump in! A beach park offers restrooms and picnic facilities, although you can turn off the road at almost any spot, park between the stately ironwoods, and find your private paradise. The reef creates a quiet lagoon, and snorkeling can be very good, though swimmers should be cautious in the shallow areas. During periods of high surf, particularly in winter, the current which runs parallel to the beach can become strong enough to pull out through the channel in the reef at the west end of the park. Swim inside the reef at all times.

Across the street, the Kauai Polo Club hosts polo matches on summer Sunday afternoons at 2 pm. You can follow the road through a quiet residential area all the way to its western end, where a stream flows into the sea. A sandbar extending quite far out invites wading and fishing. Children love the quiet water and the tiny beautiful shells along the waterline. The scene is so peaceful that you can hear an amazing combination of sounds: the roar of the surf breaking on the reef far offshore, and near your feet, the gentle rippling of the sea upon the sand.

If you begin your sunset drive to Hanalei too late to reach there before dark, you can watch the sun set into the ocean at Anini Beach, a glorious sight which can be yours in perfect solitude. The tall ironwood trees darken to feathery silhouettes against a pale gray and orange sky, filled with lines of puff clouds. The water shimmers gold as the sun's dying fire fades slowly to a pearl and smoky gray, to the songs of crickets and the lapping of gentle waves.

Kalihiwai Bay

You'll catch your first glimpse of Kalihiwai Bay as you drive down the narrow road carved into the side of the sheer cliff which encloses it on one side. From the side, the bay is a perfect semicircle of blue, rimmed with shining white sand and nestled between two lava cliffs. Ironwood trees ring the beach and behind them, across the sandy road, several homes peek out at the sea. A clear, freshwater stream flows into the bay near the far end, so shallow and gentle at low tide that small children can splash around safely. It becomes deep enough behind the beach to be the departure point for royak excursions, although swimming is not recommended in the river itself.

One of our favorite family beaches, Kalihiwai Bay offers wonderful summertime fun for people of all ages. Little ones will love the shallow pools behind the beach where they can fish or float on rafts. Ocean swimming is terrific too! The waves rise very slowly and break in long, even crests over a sloping sandy bottom, perfect for wave jumping and boogie boarding. One summer day we watched a dozen children celebrate a birthday with a surfing party. In winter, the surf and currents in the bay become formidable. Even experienced surfers may have difficulty managing the rip currents which can be particularly strong when a swell is running. If the surf is too rough, Kalihiwai is a lovely beach for walking, with firm sand and magnificent views of the cliffs.

Directions: A yellow siren atop a pole just south of the beach is a reminder of the *tsunami* or tidal wave of 1946 which washed away the bridge originally linking the two roads to the bay. Both are still marked Kalihiwai Road at their separate intersections with Rt 56. Either one will take you to the bay, although if you choose the Kalihiwai Road just north of the long bridge on Rt 56, you'll have to wade across the stream's mouth in order to reach the beach. The Kalihiwai Road south of the bridge and just north of Kilauea winds through the countryside before curving down the steep cliff on the southern edge of the bay.

Secret Beach

Secret Beach is one of those rare and special places where the world can be forgotten, where you can feel, for a few hours, as if you were alone at the beginning of time. The colors are brilliant, the breeze fresh and tangy with salt. The ocean reaches out to touch the sky at an endless horizon, and the crashing of waves is all you can hear. As you walk, you will leave the only footprints on warm, golden sand shining brilliantly in the sun.

Nestled at the base of a sheer cliff just north of Kilauea, Secret Beach is well off the beaten track for good reason. You must hike down (and back up!) a rocky trail which zigzags through trees, gullies, and brush. You can drive only to the trail's beginning at the top of the cliff. From here, you can hear the waves crashing below—apparently not very far away—which is reassuring as you look down on a trail which seems to disappear into a tangle of jungle. The path is steep in places —sneakers are a good idea— but branches, roots, and vines offer plenty of handholds, and if you're out of shape, you can always resort to the seat of your pants!

The walk down will take about seven minutes, just long enough to whet your appetite. You'll even feel rather daring as the path makes the last sharp plunge before leveling off to the sand, and you can see, at last, through a screen of palm trees and hanging vines, a magnificent stretch of golden sand and a shining turquoise sea. In rainy times, this enormous triangle of sand may be partly covered by a lagoon fed by a stream winding down behind the beach. You can walk in either direction. To the left, you can climb a rocky outcropping and find a small beach ending in a steep cliff. A house or two perched atop the cliff will startle you, although the cliff is too sheer for any trail down. To the right of the beach trail, you can walk a long way across the sand and perhaps explore some small caves etched by the waves into the base of the cliff.

Secret Beach is not a place to come alone, for the obvious reason of its isolation. Swimming is not a good idea. The surf is rough, and the current strong and unpredictable; you'd never find a lifeguard if you were caught in an undertow. In fact, during the winter, this beach, enormous as it is, can disappear almost entirely under huge, crashing waves. Instead of swimming, walk along the water, hunt for shells, and forget everything but the feel of wet sand between your toes.

The walk back up the cliff will give you time to adjust to the world you left behind—just about 10 minutes of mild exertion, with the air cool under the trees and the leaves speckled with sunlight.

This would not be a pleasant hike in the mud, though, so plan your adventure with an eye to the weather and don't go after a soaking rain. By the time you reach your car and remember that you have to stop at the store for chocolate milk, the peaceful solitude you left behind will be as hard to recapture as a wave rippling on the sand. But for a few moments, you were lost forever to your working-day world. This may be the secret of Secret Beach, and it is a secret worth keeping.

Directions: Drive north of Kilauea on Rt 56 about a half mile. Turn right onto Kalihiwai Road. Just a few feet beyond the first bend, turn right onto a dirt road which looks like a broad red gash in the landscape. Follow towards the water till it ends. Park, lock up and walk down the trail. The rest is up to you! Note: One reader discovered another secret about this beach, when she and her family reached the bottom of the trail and ran into "a long-haired young man wearing nothing but a guitar!" So be prepared for strange music!

Kilauea Bay

If you've ever had the fantasy of searching through the jungle to find a remote and hidden paradise, Kahili Beach at Kilauea Bay should be your destination. The road to this unspoiled beach tests the mettle of both car and driver with new challenges at practically every turn. Deeply rutted, even gouged in places by ditches and holes, it can turn into a quagmire in rain, but in dry weather, it can be navigated without too much difficulty by a careful driver even in a rented subcompact. Pick a dry day, and the road will add the zest of adventure and heighten the excitement of discovering, just beyond the last ditch and bunches of trailing vegetation, a bay shaped like a perfect half-moon, the deep blue water sparkling with light and the golden sand outstretched between two rocky bluffs like a tawny cat sleeping in the sun.

To get to the beach, you must wade across the Kilauea Stream which winds into the bay through dunes built up by the changing tides. The mouth of the stream changes shape each year. One year it may be shallow enough for small children to manage at low tide, but at other times you'll have to carry your youngsters on your shoulders. The width can vary from a few yards to fifty, and during stormy times when the stream floods, crossing may be difficult, even impossible. To the left of the stream, the beach ends abruptly in an old rock quarry, the original purpose for the road and now a great spot for pole fishing. To the right of the stream, the sandy beach extends a long way before ending in piles of lava rocks which children will enjoy climbing and exploring for tidal pools. Chances are you'll encounter only another person or two and can watch in solitude as the waves roll towards the beach in long, even swells, break into dazzling white crests, and rush towards shore in layers of gold and white foam.

Although the surf can be dangerously strong and the currents treacherous at certain times, particularly in winter when the beach may almost disappear beneath the crashing waves, we found the swimming safe enough in summer for our seven and ten-year-olds to surf on their boogie boards in the shallow water, although even close to shore the pull of the undertow made us watch them closely. The tiny blue Portuguese 'men o' war' are sometimes washed ashore here after a storm, so if you see any on the sand, go to another beach, for these small jellyfish pack a giant sting!

Behind the beach, the stream forms brackish pools where children can swim safely, except near the stream's entrance into the bay where the current can be swift, particularly at high tide. One August, the pools were wider than we had ever seen, like a shallow lagoon, and our family had a great time netting tadpoles. Our children preferred this beach to almost any other because of the variety of things they could do and the challenge of ripping the leaves off the branches that scraped the sides of the car as we maneuvered around the gullies on the way down and back. We loved the beach because we had it all to ourselves.

Directions: At Kilauea, turn off Rt 56 onto Kolo Road, then turn left onto Kilauea Road, and drive through the town. After you pass the Kong Lung store, take the second dirt road on the right. Follow it about a mile to the end. On the way back, stop in at the Martin Farm for papayas or at Jacques's Bakery on Oka Street for fresh wheat and molasses bread and coconut danish pastries.

Larsen's Beach

Getting to Larsen's Beach is half the fun. A right-of-way-to-beach road wanders through pastureland, where horses grazing peacefully seem sketched into a landscape portrait of meadows silvery green with waving grasses, trees and mountains in richer, darker shades, and the sky light blue with masses of white, shining clouds. At the end of the well-graded, sandy road is a small parking area and a gate leading to the top of the cliff, where the beach below seems a slender ribbon of white against the dark blue water. Although a second, smaller gate seems to direct you to the right, walking through it takes you to a steep path ending in rocks.

Instead, walk down the hillside to the left on a well worn path with a gentle slope. Even our youngest had little difficulty managing the descent or the climb back up. In fact, she accepted the job of trailblazer and earned a "pathfinder" badge for leading us back up the car again! A five-minute walk down the slope brings you to a long, lovely beach curving along the coastline and disappearing around a distant bend—perfect for lazy afternoons of beachcombing and exploring Although a rocky reef extending about 70 yards offshore seems to invite snorkeling, Larsen's Beach is one of the most dangerous on the island. Before you begin the hike down, observe the ocean carefully and locate the channel through the reef, just to the left of the rocky point where you are standing. The churning water caused by the swift current makes the channel easiest to see from this height, and once noted, it can be recognized at sea level. Once you see this channel, you can also pick out the smaller channels which cut through the reef at several other points. Swimmers and snorkelers should avoid going near any of these channels, particularly the large one, because currents can be dangerously strong and even turn into a whirlpool when the tide is going out. Remember, Larsen's Beach has no lifeguard, and help is not close by. Currents can be exceptionally treacherous at any time, but particularly in winter months, and two years ago two experienced local fishermen drowned here. The watchword is caution: swim in pairs, never go out beyond the reef, try to stay within 15 yards of the shore, and examine the surface of the water carefully to avoid swimming near a channel. If you snorkel, stay where you can stand up at will, and don't get so absorbed in looking at the fish that you lose track of where you are. Have the judgment not to go out at all if surf conditions don't seem right to you.

A trip to Larsen's Beach does not require swimming or snorkeling. If you bring reef-walking sneakers to protect your feet, you can walk around in the shallow water and watch colorful fish who don't seem afraid of people. Or walk for miles along the magnificent coastline of this picture-perfect beach. Hunt for shells, or simply lose yourself in the spectacle of nature's beauty. You will probably encounter only another person or two. The drive back is wonderful, with spectacular views of the rolling hills, lined by fences and stands of trees, and beyond them the dark and majestic mountains reaching to touch the clouds.

Directions: Take Rt 56 to the Moloa'a Sunrise Fruit Stand just south of Kilauea, and turn right onto Kuamo'o Road. Go past the Moloa'a Road turnoff for about 1.1 miles and look for a dirt road on the right. The right turn will be very sharp, and then almost immediately another beach access sign will mark the left turn onto the long, straight road to the beach. Follow to the end, and walk downhill to the left.

Moloa'a Bay

At the end of a well-graded, semi-paved road which winds for several miles through the lush green countryside, Moloa'a Bay's lovely curve of sandy beach is discovered by few tourists. As you follow the road through this quiet, rural landscape, you can hear wonderful sounds emerge from the stillness—the breeze rustling in the leaves, the chirping of insects, the snorting of horses grazing in tree-shaded meadows. At road's end, you will find a gate attached to an unfriendly looking barbed wire fence intended to discourage parking along the shoulder of the road. Walk through the gate and cross a winding, shallow stream, where our children discovered tadpoles apparently not informed that frog's eggs had hatched a month earlier everywhere else.

At this point the bay, hidden by the half dozen homes which ring the beach, suddenly comes into view—an almost dazzling half-moon of shining golden sand and turquoise water. The long, wide beach ends in grassy hills and piles of lava rocks on the left and a sheer cliff on the right. To the left, the rocks are fun to climb and search for shells and trapped fish, although this windward side of the bay is too rough for swimming and the bottom very rocky. To the right of the stream, the bay is more sheltered, with bright red and yellow catamarans pulled up on golden sand sprinkled with blue morning glories. Here the water is gentler and the bottom more sandy. In summer, swelling waves make excellent swimming for adults and children accompanied by adults. Snorkelers can swim out through the sandy corridor to the rockier part of the bay near the cliff, or float in the shallow water close to shore and dig in the sandy bottom for beautiful shells. In times of heavy surf, however, this bay, like all windward beaches, can have dangerous currents and rip tides. During these times, Moloa'a Bay is a beautiful place for walking. The peaceful solitude is filled with the sound of waves. The crystal blue water, traced with the shadowy patterns of the rocks below, stretches out to the distant horizon where pale clouds fade into a limitless sky. At 5 pm you might see a dozen horses, wandering home after another difficult day of grazing, stop at the stream for a drink or a roll in the shallows—a spectacular sight with the setting sun glistening on the water and the horses darkening slowly to silhouettes.

Directions: Take Rt 56 to the Moloa'a Sunrise Fruit Stand just south of Kilauea. Turn right on Kuamo'o Road, then right again at Moloa'a Road and follow it to the end.

Eastern Shore Beach Adventures

Anahola Bay

The beach at Anahola Bay is so long that to walk from one end to the other will take you almost an hour. The colors are magnificent, particularly as the sun is rising or in late afternoon as it moves to the west over the dark green mountains, deepening the blue of the water and the gold of the sand while brightening the tall white puff clouds until they seem to glow with light.

While the walking is spectacular, swimming can be risky, for the surf can be strong and currents powerful most of the year. At the southern end of the bay, which is more sheltered, camp shelters pretty much monopolize the shoreline, so check that area out first before you bring the family. You can also park at the mid-point, where the Anahola stream meets the sea. Children will love playing in the large shallow pools formed by the stream as it winds toward the bay, which is sometimes filled with tadpoles just slow enough to be netted by the younger set. The tiny river fish were harder to catch but fun in the trying, as were the small shrimp we discovered hiding by the grasses near the bank. The children also enjoyed making voyages of discovery on their boogie boards where the stream is deeper.

Anahola Bay is a favorite place for the whole family, and a good choice on weekends when other, more well known beaches become crowded. Watch out for the small, blue 'men o' war' jellyfish which are sometimes washed ashore after a storm. If you see them on the sand, go to another beach for the day, for the sting can be very painful.

A short drive (or long walk) north of the river will take you to Aliomanu Beach, popular with local families because its extensive offshore reef is terrific for fishing and seaweed harvesting. Snorkeling is for experts only, who should venture out if tradewinds are light and the current from the river is not strong.

For a picnic on the beach, stop at Duane's Ono Burger next to the Anahola Store just north of the turn off Rt 56 to the Beach Road. Though expensive, the burgers are imaginative creations, featuring various combinations of avocado, sprouts, vegetables, teriyaki, and various kinds of cheeses. But don't eat there; pack up and head for the beach! If possible, phone your order in ahead, for the staff runs low on manners during rush hour, and the waiting area is best described as charmless.

Directions: Turn off Rt 56 at Aliomanu Road (Just north of Duane's Ono Burger and the Anahola Store) and follow it to the mouth of the stream.

Donkey Beach

Ringed by rolling pasture crisscrossed by wire fences, Donkey Beach takes it name from its gentle, four-footed neighbors. This is a lovely and peaceful spot, a long curve of sand which ends in piles of rock on both sides. Surf and currents are strong, even in summer, and surfing is for experts. Waves rise slowly; curl in long, even swells; crest with gleaming foam, and break straight down with thunderous explosions of spray. The rhythm is hypnotic—you could watch them form and crash for hours. We saw no one in the water, though—our first hint that Donkey Beach was for sun-worshipers rather than swimmers. We soon discovered that this beach is unique—the only one we've seen on Kauai where nudity is the rule. Those on the beach were not tourists, judging from their dark allover tans. Some were more covered up than others, so you won't feel out of place if you hang onto your suit. Otherwise bring along some sunblock for parts not normally exposed! Or you may regret your frolic in the altogether when you try to sit down later on!

Directions: You can no longer drive to Donkey Beach because the cane roads are gated and locked. However, about 3/4 mile north of the mile 11 marker on Rt 56, you will see cars parked on the shoulder, next to a well-worn path leading across the cane field to the beach. (The walk would take less than ten minutes). You can request a formal permit to cross private property to gain access to the beach (all beaches on Kauai are public) by stopping off during business hours at the Lihue Plantation office at 2970 Kele St. in Lihue and filling out a short information form.

Kealia Beach

North of Kapa'a on Rt 56 and just past a scenic overlook turnout, you will see spectacular Kealia Beach, a long, wide curve of golden sand ending in a rocky point. When the surf is up, lots of surfers ride the long, even rollers. At low tide during summer months, the waves can be quite gentle, particularly at the far end of the beach where lava rocks extending into the sea create a cove where the water is quieter. This summer, Kealia became Jeremy's and Mikey's favorite beach for boogie boarding! The sandy bottom slopes so gradually that you can walk out to catch some wonderful long rides, though at times the waves can be too powerful for children (even adults). Exercise caution, particularly in winter. Surf near the boogie boarders, and watch out for the small, blue 'men 'o war' jellyfish, which wash into shore after high surf. If you see them on the sand, they are probably also floating in the water! They pack a nasty sting, so go to another beach for the day! Firm, level sand makes this a perfect walking beach, and children will enjoy playing in shallow pools behind the beach where a stream flows into the ocean. Strong rip currents near the river mouth, however, make ocean swimming hazardous. Plenty of parking is available off Rt 56.

Kapa'a Beaches

A white sandy beach, which runs almost the length of Kapa'a town, offers relatively safe swimming and fun for families with small children. An offshore reef breaks the surf and wind chop, creating a quiet lagoon, except in winter months when an eastern swell can make a strong current flow out of the channel. Usually, however, the water is calm, filled with children splashing while babies play in the shaded sand. Turn towards the water at Niu St. by Kapa'a ballpark.

Lydgate Beach Park

You can picnic, barbecue, or just come for the swimming at this wonderful park just south of the Wailua River. It's a favorite spot for families on the island's eastern shore because it has something for everyone. A rock-rimmed pool provides safe swimming for babies and toddlers, even in winter months. Adjacent is an enormous rock-rimmed pool which breaks the surf into rolling swells excellent for swimming, rafting, and floats of all kinds. The pool is one of the best year-round snorkeling spots on the island, for many brightly colored fish feed along the rocky perimeter, and the rocky wall protects swimmers from dangerous currents. If you bring along some stale bread or crackers in a plastic bag, they will swim right up to you! You can also fly a kite, play frisbee on the wide, sandy beach, collect shells and driftwood. There are showers for rinsing off sand and salt before going home.

A nice walk northward takes you around the bay to the Wailua River. Sometimes the river mouth is shallow enough to ford, but at other times it can be deep and treacherous. Swimming in the brackish, calm water of the river can be fun, although parents of young children should not let them stray from the edges because the water can become deep very quickly. Swimming where the river empties into the bay is not recommended because currents can be dangerous and unpredictable.

If you walk south from the lava pools, the beach is gorgeous and almost deserted. Continue past the rocky point in front of Kaha Lani condominiums, and you can walk all the way to the Kauai Hilton. You'll have spectacular views of the coastline, particularly when sunrise or sunset paints the sky with gold and orange, and deepens the blues of the ocean, bright with shining foam. The beach is perfect for walking, and the patterns of foam crossing the sand are the most lovely we have ever seen. You'll probably find only one or two people, probably fishermen checking their lines. Swim with caution, however, for the surf is rough and currents powerful; Lydgate's pools are much safer.

Directions: Take Leho Road off Rt 56 just north of the Wailua Golf Course. The turn to the park is clearly marked. Follow the road around to the left to get to the lava pools. If you want to walk the long end of the beach, take the first right turn instead. A long road runs along the beach, behind the Kaha Lani Condominium and the Wailua golf course, and there are plenty of places to park.

Hanama'ulu Beach

A perfect crescent of soft shining sand, the beach at Hanama'ulu Bay is perfect for building sandcastles and hunting sunrise shells. In summer, the waves are gentle enough for children to enjoy. Rolling to shore in long, even swells only about a foot or two high, they break into miniature crests which turn to layers of white foam flecked with sandy gold, like the lacy borders of a lovely shawl. Even the occasional "wipe-outs" were not serious because the sandy bottom slopes very gradually.

Children can chase lots of tiny sandcrabs, and there is plenty of shade for babies beneath the tall, graceful ironwood trees which fringe the sand. Behind the beach, the Hanama'ulu Stream forms shallow pools as it winds toward the bay, and the bottom is so firm that small children can wade, pulling toy trucks or cars behind them. Older ones can hunt for tiny crayfish and other river creatures to capture with nets. Local children like to scoot across the sandbar on handcrafted skim boards, disks of gaily colored, varnished plywood, or race their bikes along the bank and up improvised ramps in order to plunge them into the water where the stream is deeper. They also build enormous rafts of river plants and float with the current, which can begin to flow rapidly in a short time when the tide changes.

This spot behind the beach is quite beautiful. The deep gold of the river is shaded by trees so tall and dense you can hardly see the sky, and the dark green leaves trail into the water behind stalks of lavender water hyacinths, their petals streaked with the colors of peacock feathers. A picnic pavilion faces the river, and other tables look out over the beautiful curve of the bay. Everything is uncrowded, even the playground, as this beach is frequented by few tourists. Unfortunately, it is also in the path used by helicopters returning to the airport at the end of their scenic tours, and so you hear a lot of choppers. Try to ignore them, and also the semi-permanent tents of campers. Plan your visit for the morning as the mosquitoes get hungry about 4 pm!

Directions: Turn off Rt 56 towards the sea at Hanama'ulu, just north of Lihue. Bear right at the fork. The road ends at the park.

Kalapaki Beach

Kalapaki Bay is unforgettably beautiful. Almost enclosed by craggy green hillsides, this natural harbor has a wide sugar sand beach with some of the best swimming on the island. The waves roll to shore in long, even swells and break in shining white crests which are usually great for swimming and rafting. If the surf is too rough, you can stretch out on the warm, golden sand and watch brilliant red and yellow windsurfers or catamarans skim gracefully across the blue water. The horizon is fascinating. On one side, the green ridges of the mountains have the contours of a giant animal sleeping in the sun, while on the other side, houses on stilts perch so precariously on the side of a sheer cliff that you wonder what combination of faith and hope keeps them standing.

The hotel on this beach is the extraordinary Westin Kauai, which is part art museum, part tropical zoo, and part marine aquarium. Some might add, part movie set for Ben Hur filming on Gilligan's Island, for about this very controversial hotel, few people are neutral. Some people love it; others consider it completely out of place on Kauai. You'll have to make up your own mind. But here you'll find Kauai's largest swimming pool, its tallest high-rise, its largest collection of south seas art, and its only two-story escalator. You'll also find guests traveling in carriages drawn by Clydesdale horses, or in Venetian launches on man-made lagoons. Whether you like extravagance on such a spectacular scale, the beach is lovely and, like all beaches on Kauai, is public land. Kalapaki Beach is a favorite spot with our family for boogie boarding and skim boarding when the surf is relatively quiet. Be sure to heed any high surf warnings, however, for at certain times, the waves can break straight down with enormous force, and every so often a really big wave seems to come up out of nowhere to smash unwary swimmers.

    The Westin is a friendly place (Their slogan is "You don't have to check-in to check us out!"). Before or after swimming, you can hire a carriage for a tour of the grounds or take a ride by launch around the lagoon to Fashion Landing and back. Kids love it, the launch is free, and it gives you a reason to put your car in the hotel lot. Have lunch at Duke's, or walk across the street to Cafe Portofino in the Pacific Ocean Plaza, and spend the rest of the morning on the beach!

Directions: Take Rice St. through Lihue until you see the Anchor Cove Shopping Center on your left, just past the Westin main entrance. Park in the lot , as close to the water as you can. Or, drive into the Westin main entrance, pass the lobby, and take the second right. That road will take you to the public beach access parking lot behind the newest of the hotel's three towers.

Ninini Beach

    The drive to this tiny beach, "Running Waters," is more interesting than the destination. You wind along a cane road right next to the airport runway, so close, actually, that the jets taking off and landing almost make you want to duck. It's great fun having such a close–up view! Turn off Ahukini Road about a half mile after the fence at the end of the airport. The sugar cane road will be on your right, winding through brush and rustling grasses along the rocky coastline towards the lighthouse at Ninini Point. Driving the two and a half miles to the Nawiliwili Lighthouse requires maneuvering around the ruts and gullies for about 15 minutes. Walk to the lighthouse for a gorgeous view of the coast (Be careful of the footing on the rocks). Surf crashes on the rocks, and the beach is not safe for swimming; sharks have also been seen. Come instead for the view and the seclusion! You can also drive into the Westin, park in the lot by Sharky's, and walk down a path to the beach.

South Shore Beach Adventures

Maha'ulepu

At the end of a dusty drive through winding sugar cane roads, you will find a beautiful sandy beach carved into a rocky point. This part of the south shore is very dry and very hot — and you'll soon find a thin red film on every surface inside your car, including you! But it's worth the dust to reach a beach astonishing in its wild beauty, the surf crashing against the rocks and sand, the churning turquoise water almost glowing with sunlight. Beautiful it is, but not for swimming. Except for times when surf on the whole south shore is unusually flat, you'll find the waves crashing with enough force to knock you down, and currents powerful enough to make even local people wary.

Maha'ulepu is a lovely beach for exploring. On the eastern end, a lovely half-moon of golden sand nestles at the base of a rocky cliff. A long walk takes you around to the west, past a rocky reef which at low tide juts out of the sand in fascinating formations. As you reach the end of the curve, the tip turns out to be a point, and on the other side, you'll find another, even longer stretch of beach. Here the water ripples in toward shore, protected by an offshore reef where the waves roll in long, even swells. You might see a fisherman casting his line or even a swimmer snorkeling among the rocks where the water is shallow enough to stand. When the tradewinds are strong, windsurfers splash color on the sparkling sea. At the westernmost end, you will find an old plantation house and sunwarmed tidal pools with water shallow and still enough for children. Bring nets to catch the tiny fish!

At the far eastern end of the beach is a rocky bluff, great for exploring. After a moderate uphill hike, you will come to a promontory with spectacular views of the coastline. An offshore pillar of rock, eroded over centuries to an impossibly narrow base, seems ready to snap with the next crash of surf. Rock formations are astonishing, and a tiny beach set into the cliffside shelters interesting pools of tiny sea life. Don't climb the rocks, as a sudden wave could knock you off! Remember: this is a beautiful—but dangerous and isolated—place. Use caution.

Directions: Take Poipu Road past the new Hyatt Hotel. Pass the turnoff to Shipwreck Beach and continue east, past the golf course and the quarry. When you come to a stop sign, turn right and head toward the water. This is sugar company land, and you'll have to stop at a gatehouse and sign a release form to gain entry. At the end of the road, you can turn right or left, going either east or west along the beach.

Shipwreck Beach

Shipwreck Beach along Keoniloa Bay was never much of a beach—until Hurricane 'Iwa blasted the south shore of Kauai and created a new coastline. What was once a thin curve of sand is now enormous, a long, golden crescent divided by lava rocks. To the right of the rocks, the waves roll across a long, shallow reef ending in a rocky point. To the left, the wide, gleaming sand stretches to the base of a low cliff flanked by sand dunes.

This place is called Shipwreck Beach with good reason. The surf is powerful, breaking in long, shining arcs which crest slowly, one at a time, with deceptive smoothness, and then crash in thunderous explosions of spray very close to shore. Local people warn that beyond the break point are dangerous currents and large rocks. A better place for family swimming would be Poipu Beach Park, and novice surfers would be better off at Wailua Beach, where rocks and wind are not a problem. Be particularly careful, during summer months, of high surf.

Instead of swimming, you can limb the cliff to explore strange caves and rock formations. The colors are breathtaking—the deep blue of the water and the gold of the cliffs dazzle the eye, and the view down is a dizzying spectacle of surf crashing against the rocks. Be careful, though. Avoid going close to the cliff's edge, as the footing is slippery with loose sand. It's great for photographers but not for children.

Directions: To park at the beach, take Poipu Road past the main entrance to the Hyatt Hotel. Turn toward the water on Ainako Road. Park in the lot. The Hotel offers public restrooms and showers

Brennecke's Beach

Legendary for years as the best beach for body surfing, Brennecke's Beach is making a slow reappearance after being completely washed away during Hurricane 'Iwa. The giant boulders hurled into the water by the winds have almost all been removed, and the sand is building up slowly on the shore. Most important, the currents which created those wonderful long rolling waves are coming back. Some days you may see forty surfers crowding the waves! Be careful, for today the big rollers break much closer to shore and can throw your boogie board against the rocky sea wall! And every so often, a huge wave comes up, poises with glistening power and then breaks straight down. So if you see the other swimmers dive under a big wave, follow their example!

Directions: Brennecke's is adjacent to Poipu Beach Park on Ho'one Road as you drive east.

Poipu Beach Park

You could not imagine a more perfect beach for children than this lovely curve of soft golden sand sloping down to a gentle, friendly sea. The waves, with changing shades of turquoise sparkling with sunlight and dazzling white foam, break gently over a protective reef across the entrance to this small cove. For babies and toddlers, a ring of black lava rocks creates a sheltered pool where the water is shallow and still. For older children, waves beyond the pool roll to shore in graceful swells perfect for rafting, under the watchful eye of a county lifeguard. Children also love to explore the long rocky point at the far end of the beach and look for tiny fish trapped in the tidal pools. Bring nets and pails for the hunt! Restrooms, outdoor showers, barbecues, and picnic tables are available. Pavilions offer shade for babies, and swings will keep older children busy when they tire of the water. "Mama's Beach," as it is called by many local people, is perfect for families, and a great place for a sunset picnic, barbecue, or occasionally, on weekend afternoons, listening to a free concert.

Beyond the rocky point you can explore three crescent shaped, lovely sandy beaches. Just across the point in another sheltered cove fronting the Waiohai Hotel, is some of the best snorkeling on the island. Hundreds of fish in rainbow colors feed on the coral, so tame they almost swim into your hands. Carry stale bread or crackers in a plastic bag, or the snorkeling fish food available in dive shops, and they'll come right to you! Be careful not to follow the fish out too far! Stay inside the outer reef.

Further west, the beaches in front of the Kiahuna Plantation, the Poipu Beach Hotel, and the Sheraton have stronger surf, but an offshore reef breaks up the swell and creates excellent swimming. As you walk along this lovely string of beaches, it is hard to imagine that, the morning after Hurricane 'Iwa, this shoreline was completely straightened and all the sandy spits had washed away.

Since we began coming to Poipu years ago, the number of hotel rooms and apartments sharing these beaches has quadrupled. The effects of recent development are most evident at Poipu Beach Park, long a favorite of both tourists and local residents. The beach gets crowded earlier, stays crowded longer, and is much *more* crowded. Somehow, however, there always seems to be room for one more six-year-old! Come early in the morning or late afternoon, if possible.

Directions: After you pass through Koloa, bear left at the fork near the Kukuiula Stores to the Poipu Beach Road. Pass the Waiohai, turn right on Ho'owili Road then left at Ho'one Road and park in the lot next to Brennecke's, which serves good quality take-out sandwiches. To park at the other beaches, turn left off the Beach Road into the entrance of any of the hotels.

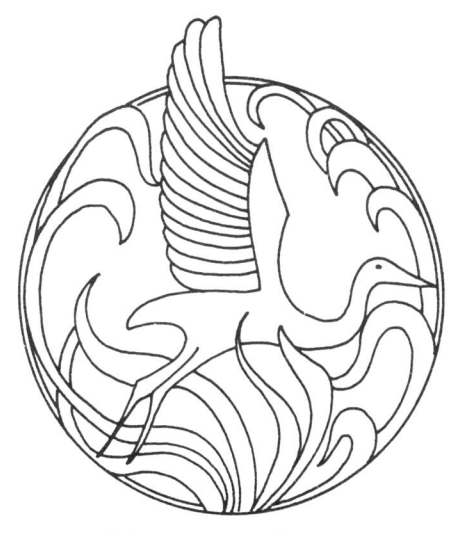

Westside Beach Adventures

Salt Pond Beach Park

What is most astonishing about Salt Pond Beach Park is the intensity of the colors—the brilliant blues of the water and sky, the bright gold of the sand, the vivid greens of sugar cane fields extending in squares and rectangles up the slopes of nearby mountains—all bathed in sunshine that makes everything sparkle. The beach is a perfect semi-circle, where the sand slopes downward with the lovely grace of a golden bowl to hold the sea. A reef near the mouth of this sheltered cove breaks the surf into slow, rolling swells that break again gently near the shore so that children can raft and swim safely inside this natural lagoon most of the year. Rock formations at both ends of the beach create large pools which are calm enough at low tide for babies and toddlers. Older children can try their luck at catching the tiny, swift fish with nets.

Walk along the beach and explore tidal pools and the ancient salt ponds where local people still harvest sea salt. The park is spectacular, especially when brightly colored windsurfers race out across the reef, and particularly favored in terms of weather. Even when clouds and rain prevail elsewhere, this little point of land seems to escape them, and in winter, the water seems a few degrees warmer and more friendly.

Showers, rest rooms, picnic tables, and barbecues make this a popular spot for local families and increasingly for tourists, particularly on weekends, although the beach never seems crowded. Be careful in periods of high surf, however, when unpredictable currents create hazardous swimming, and stay inside the lagoon. On the way home, stop at the Green Garden Restaurant for fabulous coconut cream or *lilikoi* chiffon pies.

Directions: Turn onto Rt 543 at Hanapepe, take the first right onto Lokokai Rd, and drive until you see the parking area.

Waimea Black Sand Beach

Just off the main street of Waimea town is a long beach, and unusual on Kauai, this one is black sand. The beach looks eerie, as if dusted with coal, and the water is dusky. A recreational fishing pier extends out into the ocean, and along the beach, restored plantation cottages afford a glimpse of what life was like when sugar was king. In this quiet spot, you can wander along the beach and invent stories — perhaps an angry goddess, jealous of the sun mirrored so brightly on the surface of the sea, tried to darken the water and sand with ash from her volcano.

Directions: Between the mile 22 and 23 markers on Rt 50 in the town of Waimea, turn towards the ocean until you find Lau Road. Follow to the end.

Pakala's, or Infinities

On this lovely, curving beach, the sand and sea are deep gold, as if sprinkled with cinnamon, because the A'akukui stream carries red sugar cane soil to the sea. As you walk from the road across private pastureland, you can hear the crash of the waves before you can see the beach, and by the time you pass through the trees which ring the sand, you'll feel you're on a desert island with no people in sight.

It is a lovely spot. The waves rise gracefully in long, even lines crested with gold. Each wave breaks and rushes onto the sand in shining foam, and then it rolls back out again to meet the wave coming in. In a fascinating ballet, the waves sometimes meet like dancers in perfect rhythm, and shining spray bursts into the air as they join. Sometimes the waves clash or collide, but there's a beauty even in this more dissonant rhythm. Although you could watch the waves for hours, you would never see two waves embrace in exactly the same way.

The bay is divided by a rocky point where local fishermen try for pompano. If you cross the stream and climb the rocky ledge, you come to a sandy beach with lots of shells, sea glass, and coral. Beyond the reef is a summertime surfing spot famous for long, perfectly formed waves that surfers can ride on to "infinity." Paddling out over the shallow reef takes a long time, but the ride, according to our son Jeremy, is well worth it! Be careful at low tide, when shallow water over the reef which can expose an unwary surfer to spiny sea urchins.

To the right of the rocky point, the beach stretches a long way before disappearing around a bend. The firm golden sand is perfect for walking, and the waves can be quite gentle. This western spot is a great place to try when other parts of the island are in rain.

Directions: Drive north on Rt 50 past the mile 21 marker. Look for a low concrete bridge and a level area on the shoulder of the road for parking. Next to the bridge over the A'akukui Stream, an overgrown path leads through pasture to the beach. Wear sturdy sandals and stay away from the thorny *kiawe* which grows near the beach. About 1 mile north on Rt 50 are public restrooms, and a bit further, just across the Waimea River, you'll find public showers.

Kekaha Beaches

Stretching for miles along Kauai's western coast, the Kekaha beaches combine swimming, surfing, and walking with the predominantly dry weather of the island's leeward side. As Rt 50 curves toward the sea at the small town of Kekaha, the beach is narrow, but a mile or two north, it widens and becomes more golden, with long, rolling waves breaking evenly in brilliant white crests. At times, the soft breaking waves can be perfect for boogie boards, although, as everywhere on Kauai, surf and currents can be dangerous and unpredictable. During winter months, you may find high surf and rip currents. Watch where local people are swimming and follow their example!

At several places along the road, stands of trees provide shade for babies. We recommend driving the full length of this stretch of beach so that you can select the most favorable spot and then double back to park. Despite its clear, sunny weather, the western side of the island has not yet been developed as a tourist area, and so these beaches are frequented primarily by local residents and are not very crowded. You can walk for miles along the sand, with beautiful views of Ni'ihau, purple on the horizon. Or drive north towards Barking Sands and Polihale Beach, winding through sugar cane fields where silvery grasses wave in the breezes against the deep red-gold of cleared fields and the vivid blues of the sea and the enormous sky.

Barking Sands

South of Polihale, the sandy beach continues for about 15 miles, and the section off Barking Sands Missile Range is often available for public use. Call 335-4111 in advance to be sure that the area has not been closed for maneuvers! After signing in at the main gate, you can drive to a long stretch of sandy beach along Major's Bay. Like Polihale Beach, the surf here can be extremely strong, often too powerful for safe swimming, particularly in winter. While the waves break magnificently in long, shining tunnels that look like a surfer's dream, unpredictable currents as well as a sudden drop-off make for particularly hazardous swimming conditions. You have to look carefully for channels through the coral reef fronting the beach to find sandy bottom, or you can go to the northernmost point of Major's bay where the reef ends. The wide, sandy beach is both hot and difficult to walk on, and shade is almost nonexistent. It is a spectacular place for a picnic, though, and you can see Ni'ihau, purple on the horizon, just past the golden, shining sand and glistening turquoise sea.

Polihale Beach

From the time you leave paved road behind to jolt north through a maze of sugar cane fields, you know you're in for something extraordinary. Gradually, beyond the tall sugar cane rustling in the breeze, a dark ridge of jagged peaks appears on the right. As you get closer, these giant cliffs reveal splendid colors— trees and bush in vivid greens against the black rock slashed with the deep red of the volcanic soil. When you can drive no further, the beach at Polihale emerges from the base of the cliffs—an enormous stretch of brilliant white sand more immense, it seems, than the cliffs which tower above and the band of deep blue sea beyond. Only the sky seems the equal of this vast expanse of glaring sand, so wide that to walk from your car to the ocean on a sunny day will burn your feet, and so long that no single vantage point allows the eye to see its full extent. "Beautiful" is too small a word for this awesome place. Polihale—home of spirits—is more appropriate, not only because the majestic cliffs and beach dwarf anything human to insignificance, but also because here man's access to the north coast really ends. Beyond lies the Na Pali wilderness, unreachable except by boat or helicopter, or by the handful of hikers who dare to climb the narrow and dangerous trails. Polihale is the threshold between the known and the unknown, the tamed and the untamed, the familiar and the wild.

The swimming here is treacherous; the rolling, pounding surf even at its most gentle is only for strong, experienced swimmers. No reefs offer protection from the powerful ocean currents. Come instead for the spectacle, to picnic and walk, to gaze at the grandeur of the cliffs above the endless sea and sand, to listen to the silence broken only by the crashing surf, to appreciate in solitude the splendor of nature's power. A feeling of awe lingers even after you return to paved road and a world of smaller proportions.

Directions: Just before Rt 50 ends, a State Park sign will mark the left turn onto the dirt cane road. Follow signs for about 5 miles to the parking area.

Beach Safety

We describe the beaches in their summer mood, when the surf and currents can be at their most gentle. From mid-October to mid-April, however, swimmers must be particularly cautious on the windward beaches to the north and northeast where the surf and currents are more unpredictable and dangerous. On the south shore, surf is "up" in summer months. Plan your beach adventures according to surf conditions (Call 245-6001 for a report on the size of the swell and the times of high and low tides).

A few simple suggestions: Don't swim alone or too far out at a beach where the currents are unfamiliar, and avoid swimming where a river flows into the sea. Should you ever find yourself caught in a strong undertow or rip tide, and if your efforts to free yourself are not successful, remember this: don't panic, conserve your energy and drift with the current until it weakens. These currents usually weaken beyond the point where the waves break, and many are shaped like horseshoes, so that at some point you will probably be able to swim back in.

Be particularly careful when you are snorkeling, when you can easily get distracted by the fish and lose your sense of direction. Stay close enough to shore that you can swim (or walk!) in at any time, and remember that unfamiliar beaches will have unknown currents. You'll find the safest snorkeling in the rock-enclosed pool at Lydgate Park on the eastern shore, or at sheltered Poipu Beach to the south. Snorkelers should avoid using reef walking slippers weighted with lead; when soaked, these slippers can become heavy enough to pull you down.

Beware of walking or even standing close to the edge of cliffs or rocks to photograph the pounding surf, as waves vary in size and strength and a huge one may come up suddenly and wash your camera away—perhaps you along with it! These sudden large waves can be treacherous because they are unexpected as well as powerful, particularly on northern and western beaches where there are no reefs to protect against strong ocean currents.

When surfing, watch where the local surfers ride the waves. They know where the currents are too strong, and where the wave break is too dangerous for safe riding. Keep an eye out for that occasional oversize wave. Rather than trying to ride it, you may want to dive through or drop down under it. These big ones often come in threes, so be ready!

The Portuguese 'man o' war', a tiny blue jellyfish, packs a huge walloping sting in its long, trailing tentacle. They sometimes dot the waterline after being washed ashore by heavy surf. Don't step on them or pick them up. If you are stung while swimming, pull the jellyfish off carefully, trying not to touch the stinger any more than you have to, or use some sand to scrape the stinger off. Meat tenderizer is sometimes used as a poultice to help break down the poison. The best medicine, however, is prevention. If you see them on the sand, pack up and head out for another beach! An even smaller critter, the bacterium *leptospirosis*, has been found in Kauai's rivers and streams, so avoid fresh-water swimming if you have open cuts or sores. Instead, swim in the ocean or the brackish water where a stream flows into the sea.

Your beachbag should contain some antibiotic ointment and bandaids for coral cuts, and, if possible, some meat tenderizer. A spare sun tan lotion in the glove compartment or the car is also a good idea.

On Kauai, as anywhere, follow normal rules of self-protection: Lock your car against theft as you would at home, and avoid walking alone at night in unlit, deserted areas—including those romantic beaches.

```
Weather & Surf
   245-6001
```

Restaurants

North Shore, 49
Eastern Shore, 70
South Shore, 124
Westside, 146

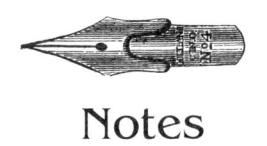

Notes

North Shore Restaurants

Bali Hai

Imagine dining as the sunset paints the sky all gold and orange above the magnificent angles of the dark and mysterious mountains, turning the ocean almost purple in Hanalei Bay. Sip a cocktail while the cool evening breeze, fragrant with tropical flowers, touches your skin like silk. At the Bali Hai Restaurant, you can find the Kauai of your imagination, the dream of an island paradise that haunts you in the dead of winter. The dining experience could not be more relaxing, with the food brought at a leisurely pace by polite waiters and served on large, elegantly appointed tables. Open to the air on three sides, the dining room has high ceilings and a two-tiered arrangement of tables which makes the room spacious and, even when full, remarkably quiet. As we lingered over coffee to watch a sudden shower fill the air with shining drops, we felt more at peace than when we arrived.

The recently completed renovation of the Hanalei Bay Resort has had great results for Bali Hai. Finally, the design has taken full advantage of the view, and your line of vision is above the lanai railing, thanks to taller chairs. Even better, directly below the dining room, a wonderful salt water pool meanders through tropical gardens. Instead of tennis courts lit for night games, you can look out at the flowers and palm trees and listen to the sound of waterfalls instead of tennis balls.

All the ingredients for a fantastic restaurant, one would think. But perhaps some *kapuna* haunts the kitchen, for in more than ten years of dining at Bali Hai, we have always found it difficult to find something good to eat while we occupied a table and enjoyed the sunset. In fact, over the years this restaurant has had several new owners, chefs, and menus, and we have marveled at how so many could fail with so spectacular a dining room!

Our most recent dinner was the best in years! The fresh *ahi* ($21) was excellent, almost the size of a NY steak, and both moist and tender, although the Thai sauce which came with was fairly peppery, so you might take the precaution of having it served on the side. The filet mignon ($23.50) was tasty if not exceptional. Best was the rack of lamb ($23.50), two enormous chops perfectly cooked, moist and flavorful.

Dinner begins with a generous basket of *lavosh*, served with honey tarragon butter. For an even better combination of flavors, ask for a serving of curry and coconut sauce (served with shrimp cocktail) to dip it in! Spicy shrimp soup was delicious, the broth seasoned with lemon grass and each bowl filled with large size shrimp and straw mushrooms, almost like a shrimp cocktail as a soup! Or you can choose the reasonably priced, reasonably sized dinner salad.

The menu is not inexpensive. About a dozen full dinners are priced from $17.50 (*teriyaki* chicken) accompanied by soup or salad, a vegetable, and rice or potatoes, as well as four "Lite Fare" choices from $13.50 (vegetable stir fry). Still on the menu, despite all the management and ownership changes during the last ten years, is salmon in crust, which we have come to regard as an old friend, though now priced at a whopping $21.50. The wine list, which used to be both small and expensive, is now small but reasonably priced, with some good choices for around $20, including Chalone's less expensive label white table wine, Gavilan ($21).

Or come for lunch and enjoy the view in sunlit splendor. The menu offers salads and sandwiches served with french fries, fruit or cottage cheese. Thai chicken salad ($8.75) is generous with chunks of chicken, both dark and white meat, lots of vegetables and nuts, and a mild, tasty sesame dressing. The huge club sandwich ($8.75) features lots of turkey and ripe tomatoes. Crispy chicken ($8) is served piping hot on a platter with lettuce and tomato, and the hamburger ($7), while not huge, is perfectly cooked and tasty.

Bali Hai has a wonderfully romantic ambiance and unmatchable view. Even if the food were terrible, it would still be worth the price of admission. You'll enjoy your evening if you stick to the basics and don't ask the kitchen for fancy footwork. Time your dinner for just before sunset, have all sauces served in a side dish, and hope for the best!

When making dinner reservations, ask to speak directly with the *maitre de*; that way you can avoid arriving at the restaurant to find no record of your call. Even if that should happen, do not despair. You can discover, as we did, a wonderful walk to a new lookout point for the sunset. Head towards the cliff along the sidewalk between the tennis courts. From path's end, you can look down at Hanalei Bay, sparkling with beads of light and turning deep purple as the sun descends. A sailboat cuts silently across the water, the sails filling with the breezes which brush your face and fill your head with the fragrance of evening flowers. The cliffs are like dark velvet, their sharp craggy edges blended by the sun's magic into soft purples and deep blues. The gold and orange sun slowly sinks towards the water, shining more brightly with each second, until flattened by the sea into a disk that shrinks to nothing before your eyes. A golden glow remains, burnishing the clouds, polishing the water, then slowly fades into a darkening dusk.

In Princeville. Reservations: 826-7670. Credit cards. House wine: Inglenook ($9). Coffee: $1. Children's entrees (steak, chicken, mahi mahi) 25% off adult prices. Dinner 5:30-10 pm. Lunch 11:30 am - 2 pm. Map: 6

Beamreach

For years, this small, unpretentious restaurant tucked away in the Pali Ke Kua condominium at Princeville has served the most superb filet mignon the island has to offer. A full two inches thick, this 12 oz steak is perfectly cut and perfectly cooked, at once tender and crisp, juicy and flavorful—a steak worth writing a postcard home about! Although a change in ownership during 1989 had everyone worried, the new owners are committed to the same high standards that have made the Beamreach special. Wichita beef is still flown in fresh twice, even three times a week, and the family-style salad bowl and baked potato are still included in the dinner price. In fact, the kitchen and dining staff is largely unchanged.

In addition to the outstanding steaks ($23.50), the menu features more reasonably priced dinner choices like an outstanding chopped sirloin, an enormous 10 oz portion as tasty as it is generous ($14.95), boneless teriyaki chicken breasts ($12.95), or chili ($10.95). Unlike many restaurants, Beamreach manages to excel in both steak and fresh fish, for the fresh *mahi mahi* ($19.50) has the color, taste and flaking texture of magical timing. The fresh *ahi* and the fresh *ono* have also been perfectly cooked despite the thickness of the generous filets. Lobster tail is another excellent choice, broiled crisp and at the same time moist and tender. The portion is enormous! Whatever's left will make a great lunch the next day, or you can order a half portion (a single tail) instead.

Entrees are accompanied by rice or a full-size, delicious baked potato, as well as warm cracked-wheat and honey bread. While at many other restaurants, we have watched the salad shrink as produce prices have grown over the years, at the Beamreach you will find a large, family style salad bowl, topped with excellent dressings, including a fine creamy Italian. At $5.95 for a bowl, the seafood chowder is thick rather than creamy. The wine list is small and inexpensive, with half the sixteen choices $20 or less. Finish off the meal with ice cream sundaes of generous scoops of Haagen Dazs or Meadow Gold ($3). Service is friendly, and children are given a full dinner at a good price: hot dog ($5.50), chicken ($6.95), and 5 oz filet ($6.95).

'Beamreach,' as the menu explains, refers to sailing before the swiftest wind, and the restaurant cues its decor to this nautical theme. The dining room is lovely in an understated way, with captain's chairs and polished wood tables lit romantically with candles. Regrettably the dining room lacks an ocean view—the only water you can see is in the apartment swimming pool. Come instead for great beef and the relaxed, intimate ambiance, and watch spectacular sunsets from the grounds outside before dinner.

In Princeville. Reservations necessary. 826-9131. Children's dinners ($4.50-10.50). Credit Cards. Map: 6

Cafe Hanalei, Princeville Resort Hotel

You could not imagine a more spectacular spot for breakfast than Cafe Hanalei, with its panoramic view of a bay that in any weather has the romantic beauty of a fairy tale. Even in the rain, you can watch the mountains peek out from veils of mist like shy princesses. Or watch as the sun's sorcery transforms the landscape from smoky greys into blazing colors—vivid greens and golds, brilliant blues, and on the mountains rising majestically above the bay, the shining silver ribbons of waterfalls. In this land of enchantment, each moment reveals a new mystery, and under the spell of such beauty, you could enjoy breakfast with only a chair!

The breakfast buffet will draw you indoors with its generous display of fruits, juices, and fresh baked pastries, blintzes with sour cream, even an omelette bar where you can have your eggs whipped into colorful and tasty creations right before your eyes. While expensive ($17.50), the breakfast buffet combines an incomparably beautiful setting with delicious food and friendly, polite service. Where else could you find such radiance in the rain?

Or come for lunch, when you can enjoy the view along with an attractive selection of sandwiches, salads, and pastas. Maui onion soup is tasty with melted cheese. While some pastas tend to be heavy on the seasoning, the sandwiches are tasty, and the child's size pizza roll is made to order.

At dinner, the setting sun kindles the sky to flame in orange and turquoise behind the darkening cliffs. Later, as Hanalei Bay recedes into the velvet darkness, tall windows mirror dozens of dancing candle flames. Tables generously spaced for private conversation are beautifully dressed with damask cloths, elegant china and sparkling crystal and silver.

All this romance is expensive. A dozen dinner entrees range from $18.50 (chicken breast) to $39 (steamed lobster) and reflect a contemporary interest in the flavors of the Pacific Rim. On the appetizer menu, for example, grilled *opakapaka* is served with black bean butter and crispy leeks ($10), or you can choose rice noodles with *shiitaki* mushrooms ($7). Marinated beef salad with yoghurt and fennel ($9.50) was elegantly presented, the beef paper thin, rare, and flavorful. Or try the chilled lobster and canteloupe bisque ($6.50), lightly creamy and not overly sweet, or the soup of the day ($4.75), in our case a very tasty bean and tomato soup. You may find the entrees somewhat disappointing in comparison. Neither the coffee-roasted rack of lamb ($26.50) nor the prime rib was sufficiently tender. Fresh fish was a better choice, the poached *onaga* ($22) perfectly cooked, though overpowered by a somewhat salty saffron almond broth served with it. Best was the *opakapaka*, which was expertly sauteed, perfectly flaky and tender.

Service is friendly and attentive, and everything is arranged to make your evening pleasant. The best part remains the setting, and it is spectacular enough to make dinner an unforgettable experience. Walk around the hotel after dinner, take the elevator down to the beach and listen to the music of the waves and the melodies of the evening breezes.

In The Princeville Hotel. Open daily.
Reservations 826-9644.
Credit cards. Coffee $2.

Cafe Zelo's Deli & Expresso Bar

Cafe Zelo's looks and tastes very much like California. The dining room shines in cheerful white, with green leafy plants hanging on rafters and colorful abstract paintings on whitewashed walls. Light blue formica tables and blond rattan chairs look clean and inviting, and behind the grey and white counter, a shining copper expresso machine presides over the proceedings, its image resplendent in the mirrored wall behind.

Cafe Zelo's offers an upscale pasta *cum* delicatessen menu, with most lunch items priced around $5 and most breakfast choices at around $4. In addition to pastas, salads and sandwiches, you'll find a variety of Lion brand coffees and wonderful steamed beverages as well as croissants and pastries. One dismal afternoon we found the spinach lasagne hot, moist and tasty, the spinach still green. Chicken *fajitas* sizzled cheerfully in the pan, with lots of celery, onions and carrots in a rather peppery sauce, alongside bowls of grated cheddar and sour cream. The roast beef sandwich, however, was thin on meat and heavy on lettuce and alfalfa sprouts.

Service was slow, primarily because we drew a waitress who seemed stuck in perpetual slow motion. Perhaps, like many things, she would have been less limp in the sunshine!

In the Princeville Shopping Center. Open daily 8 am- 6 pm (3 pm on Sundays). 826-9700. Map: 6

Casa di Amici

It's an out of the way spot for an Italian restaurant—even on Kauai. You'll find Casa di Amici in the middle of sugar cane fields and papaya groves, on the back streets of Kilauea, a former sugar plantation town which still seems closer to Kauai's past than its present. Yet this dining room would be attractive anywhere—with fresh grey and white paint, a bright red tin roof, and sliding glass doors that open to evening breezes. In the candlelight, the dark green tables, rimmed with tan and colorful with red ginger blossoms, look romantic, and the rather spare decor has a charm all its own. The menu offers something for everyone no matter how hungry. Seven pastas come in 'light or full' portions ($9 or $12), and can be served with your choice of five sauces, so pasta can either begin or end your meal, depending on your appetite. Four of the eleven veal, fish, and chicken entrees have the same price structure, and even the light portion is a generous size. You can choose from more than fifty Italian wines, with many less than $20, and the staff is well-informed about the selections.

The dining room operation—ambiance, menu, and service—is excellent . A new chef, imported from New Orleans, is improving the kitchen as well. Minestrone ($3.00), for example, is a richer, more interesting soup, with a rich tomato broth, colorful with carrots and still crunchy bell peppers and served in a tall crock to keep it hot. The small *antipasto* is generous for the modest price ($5). *Cannelloni* ($9/appetizer), two thin and elegant crepes, is presented with a deliciously light cream sauce as well as a pungent tomato sauce.

On our most recent visit, however, the entrees were disappointing. *Braciole di manzo* ($17), a roulade of beef stuffed with cheese and spices, was overcooked and overwhelmed with tomato sauce. In *Pasta Nero*, the ingredients (Italian sausage, *coppacola*, roasted bell peppers and Romana cheese sauce with crushed red chiles) seemed to be a muddle of flavors rather than a subtle blending. Less heavy-handed was chicken *cacciatora* ($10/$16), though the chicken itself was somewhat soggy. Best was the fresh fish, both moist and flaky. You might ask to have your fresh fish filet plainly sauteed, with the 'Sicilian style' tomato and onion sauce served in a side dish so you can decide for yourself how much—if any—to use! You'll love the fresh baked bread, plain or tangy with garlic.

Casa di Amici has no children's menu, and so at the minimum a child's bowl of spaghetti with meat balls will cost $9, and a coke will be $1 more. Families might try Casa Di Amici for lunch instead, for the lunch menu has a good selection of reasonably priced sandwiches and salads, lunch plates and "authentic East Coast submarines" on homemade bread.

Kauai has few Italian restaurants with as pretty a setting as this one. As the name suggests, Casa di Amici is a friendly place, and you really want the restaurant to succeed. Give it a try, order the 'light' portions, and hope for the best!

In Kong Lung Center, Kilauea, on the Lighthouse Road. Reservations 828-1388. Coffee $1. Map: 6

Charo's

As we've all discovered halfway into at least one movie or night club performance, the show is not always worth the price of admission. Looking at Charo's sleek interior, you expect a professional food operation, but what you find is high prices, uneven quality, and service so bumbling that you wonder just what business the waiter is really trying to break into.

The north shore is an expensive place to run a business. Labor is hard to find; those narrow winding roads and one lane bridges make deliveries expensive. Charo's has tried over the past few years to find a menu to satisfy the accountant as well as the customers.

The newest menu— Mexican—seems the most successful. Mexican entrees served with beans and rice are priced at $9.95, including an excellent *chimichanga*. Mesquite broiled fresh *ahi* tostada ($11.95) was delicious, though it would have been tastier (& healthier!) with fresh tomatoes instead of sour cream. Children can order an adult sized *quesadilla*, *tostada*, or *taco* with rice and beans for the child's price ($4.50), or a 1/3 pound burger with fries ($5.95). On the happy hour menu, you'll find two great lunch choices, the 'chicken fingers' ($5.95) five crispy breast strips which Lauren ranks right up there with Burger King's, and nachos (from $5.75). Portions are on the small side, so you might order some extras to round out the plates.

Service can be as variable as the food. Once we waited (not so quietly) for a full 25 minutes in a restaurant two-thirds empty, while on another visit, our food was served quickly and efficiently. On our most recent visit, the hostess was so unfriendly that we wondered if she had been marinated along with the *teriyaki* chicken.

Charo's is a pretty place. The setting, tucked into the magnificent Haena coast looking out over the waves, is hard to equal. Dining is very pleasant in two attractive rooms decorated in bamboo and rattan, with abundant ferns and hanging plants. Skylights bring in the sunshine, which gleams on the shiny tile floor (You may even need sunglasses for summertime lunches!)

Charo's seems to have fallen victim to the curse of high overhead. Perhaps it is simply not possible to offer reasonably-priced dining so far up the winding narrow road with one-lane bridges, especially when many dinner customers don't want to drive those winding narrow roads after dark! While the new Mexican menu is a definite improvement, it's still high on price and small on portions. So if your children are sandy and hungry after a hard morning at the north shore beaches, and if they beg you to pull up in front Charo's, you might just close your ears, pass out the potato chips, and drive a few miles more for lunch at Tahiti Nui or Chuck's!

Adjacent to Hanalei Colony Resort, Haena. Reservations 826-6422. Lunch 11:30 am to 3 pm. Dinner 5:30 pm to 10 pm daily. Children's menu (under 12). Map: 6

Chuck's Steak House

People who live on Kauai seem to like Chuck's in Hanalei even though (or perhaps, even because) it looks more like a mainland restaurant than a tropical island hideaway. When you walk through the door, you could be in Chuck's in West Haven, Connecticut, one of nearly fifty Chuck's Steak Houses which have opened nationwide over the last 20 years. Each is supposed to have the special identity that comes with individual ownership. But the name says it all. This is not Ernie's but Chuck's, and to our mind a chain is a chain is a chain. This happens to be a good chain, but don't expect a unique cuisine, or personalized, attentive service. For example, if you don't specifically request pacing the dinner, your entree will arrive when you've barely finished your salad. And don't expect distinctive decor. Fly fans hum on open-beamed ceilings, and candles glow on polished tables in dark booths, but two weeks after your visit you will probably not be able to remember many details of the interior, except that it was carpeted and comfortable. That is, unless you are seated on the porch, which seems to be a great deal cooler and more desirable until the mosquitoes attack!

Prices are reasonable and menu choices extensive. More than 25 entrees range from $12.50 (barbecued beef ribs) to $18.95 (11-13 oz prime rib), including 4 children's dinners from $7.50 (teriyaki chicken) to $10.95 (prime rib). Dinners include rice, warm bread and butter, and a visit to the salad bar, a modest affair of romaine and tomatoes, a few fresh vegetables and prepared salads, and excellent dressings, including an excellent best blue cheese. Go early and take some homemade cracker bread to munch on with your cocktails or wine. The wine list is limited in choice but reasonable in price.

Over the years, we have found dinners at Chuck's to be reasonably priced and reliably well-prepared. Barbecued beef ribs ($12.50) are enormous, served with a flavorful sauce, and not overly fatty. The New York steak (12 oz for $17.50) was excellent, very tender and juicy with great flavor and no gristle. The kitchen will prepare it with teriyaki sauce upon request.

Families might try Chuck's for lunch. Hamburgers ($5.95) are a third of a pound and delicious, and kids will like the hot dog ($2), which according to our twelve-year-old Mikey, was crispy and tender and "soft all around." Our prime rib sandwich ($7.75), though not as well-trimmed as it might have been, was tasty, moist, and miraculously medium-rare, served with a sauce that made it come alive. Barbecue ribs are another good choice ($5.60 for 2 ribs or $7.60 for 3 ribs). Though on one visit, the deep fryer was on the blink and we couldn't have french fries ($1 extra with sandwiches), a cheerful waitress brought us plates of chips on the house. Keep in mind that kids' sodas are priced from the bar ($1.25 each).

Lunches and dinners at Chuck's will be reasonably priced and probably reasonably good. Chuck's does not try to achieve anything spectacular or to create a unique cuisine. On the other hand, you don't get anything special either, in food or ambiance. Chuck's offers no views of Hanalei's magnificent mountains or valleys to paint a memory for dark winter evenings back home. Its reputation among local people may have something to do with that. Unlike many of us, who dream of vacationing on Kauai, perhaps they dream of vacationing in West Haven, Connecticut.

In Princeville Center, Hanalei. Reservations 826-6211. Credit cards. Coffee/brewed decaf $1.25. House wine: Round Hill $9/$5. Lunch 11:30 am- 2:30 pm. 6 pm- 10:00 pm daily. Map: 6

Foong Wong

The drive north to Hanalei for dinner, we have always believed, is spectacular enough to be worth any meal, whatever the quality. That faith has been sorely tried by our dinners at Foong Wong, where despite generous portions, the dishes are bland bordering on tasteless. Wor wonton soup ($5.95), for example, arrives at your table in a gorgeous, steaming tureen packed with miniature corn ears, pork, shrimp, carrots, straw mushrooms, and won tons. But as far as flavor goes, you could be drinking water.

Another time we tried Foong Wong for lunch, and we brought the children along for a wider range of opinion. But the cooking was almost equally disappointing, the seasoning either non-existent or heavy with salt. The pot stickers were deep fried, almost like egg rolls, with a rather tasteless filling. A better choice was the crisp *gau gee*, a portion of ten for $4.75. Best was the *saimin* ($2.95), which the children devoured to the last noodle. The kitchen usually features a fresh catch, like a Pacific lobster or a local fish called *minpori*, stir fried in a sauce which tends toward the pasty and can be full of chunks of ginger too small to pick out and too large to ignore. Even the pan-fried cake noodle ($7.50), which we have enjoyed on past visits, was overly salty this time around, although it still looked lovely, the thin noodles crisp fried into a cake, cut in squares and garnished with broccoli, carrots and mushrooms.

There's nothing special about the setting. While clean and bright, Foong Wong looks rather like a cafeteria. Parquet floors, louvered windows, brown formica tables and red folding chairs provide the color scheme; the decor is a combination of plants, red Chinese lanterns, and a 7-Up clock. A bamboo fence, complete with a few branches and leaves, divides the restrooms from the rest of the dining room and complements the bamboo arch, lit with Christmas lights, over the entrance. It's so quiet that older folks like to spend the afternoon sipping tea and reading novels to the hum of the fans, hopefully not disturbed by a group of boisterous short persons engaged in a vocal count of fried noodles in the interest of numerical equality.

At Foong Wong, you'll find the food at best inoffensive, and it's a shame, for the people are usually pleasant, it offers full bar service, and it's the only Chinese restaurant on the north shore. But if you have an uncontrollable yen for Chinese, and if your car has broken down in Hanalei, you might give serious thought to a can of Chun King!

Ching Young Shopping Center, Hanalei. 826-6996. Credit cards. Monday 5 pm to 9 pm. Tuesday - Sunday 11 am to 9 pm. Map: 6

Hanalei Dolphin

The Dolphin has always had the reputation of serving the finest seafood on the north shore. Service is friendly and leisurely in the softly lit dining room, slightly warm from the open grill in the rear. The decor is rustic, quaint without appearing contrived. Wooden shutters are raised to let in evening breezes, and lanterns glow pleasantly on polished table tops. Hope that the rock music tapes have been turned off so you can enjoy the sounds of the crickets!

The small restaurant is almost always crowded, but if you choose a weeknight and arrive around 7 pm, you shouldn't have a long wait. Even better, arrive earlier, leave your name with the hostess, and drive a few blocks to Hanalei Bay and watch the sunset. By the time you get back to the Dolphin, your table should be ready! The Dolphin, if you haven't already guessed, is a favorite destination for our spectacular sunset drives north from Wailua!

Over the past few years, if we have had an occasional disappointing dinner at the Dolphin, we have chalked it up to bad luck in the kitchen. According to our waiter, two and sometimes three chefs alternate during the week, and so the cooking inevitably varies. One night, broiled fresh *ono* filets we ordered came out partially raw, an error easily corrected. On another visit, the *ono* (a 12 oz filet for $24) was perfectly cooked— moist, tender, and flaky—cleanly broiled, with no taste of the grill. The *ahi teriyaki* ($24) is always a winner, and it remains one of the most delicious fish dinners on Kauai—juicy, tender, and full of spark. Fresh fish is Dolphin's specialty! New York steak ($18) was small and outstandingly ordinary, although *teriyaki* "Hawaiian" chicken ($14/adults; $7/children) received high marks from our kids for taste and tenderness.

Dinners come with fresh hot bread from Jacques's bakery in Kilauea, and a big bowl of delicious green salad with cherry tomatoes, bean sprouts, and choice of oil and vinegar, or creamy garlic or Russian dressings. For $9 you can have a "light dinner" of broccoli casserole or seafood chowder, served with salad, rice or french fries, and bread. Seafood chowder (also *a la carte* for $5), is creamy, steamy, full of fish, scallops, clams and potatoes, and the steak fries are (usually) thick, hot, and crispy. Baked potato is $1.50.

The wine list is very well-selected, with lots of choices in the moderate range, like a Guenoc North Coast Chardonnay for $23. Even better, our bottle was presented in a bucket filled to the top with water and ice so that the wine was perfectly chilled. We were sad to discover that an old friend on the wine list—the bottle of Chateau Lafitte Rothschild, which survived Hurricane *I'wa* even when the roof did not — was no longer available for $200. Suddenly, we felt older.

The Dolphin is a local favorite for good reason, so arrive before 7 pm or the line will be out the door and growing by the quarter hour. The setting is pleasant, the seafood usually delicious, service for the most part friendly, and, if you are staying to the south, it's a wonderful opportunity to drive north for the sunset. Just warn the waiter that any overcooked fish will be thrown back, if not into the ocean, at least onto his tray!

On Rt 56 in Hanalei, just past Princeville and the bridge over the Hanalei River. No reservations. To see who's cooking, call 826-6113. Children's dinners: chicken or steak ($7.00) shrimp ($8.50). Coffee $1.   Map: 6

Sunset Drive to Hanalei

If your accommodations are on the eastern shore, consider dinner in Hanalei, for the drive north as the sun begins to set is an experience not to be missed! Check the paper for the exact time of sunset, which may be earlier than you expect because the state of Hawaii never changes to daylight savings time. Plan to reach Hanalei about ten minutes before sunset so that you have time to park and ready your camera and are assured a spectacular drive north.

As you begin the drive, hundreds of clouds, already tinged with peach and gold, float in an azure sky above a shimmering sea. Rt 56 winds through the countryside and along the coast, with fields of sugar cane turning silver, and the colors of land and sky changing almost mile by mile as the declining sun deepens the greens and blues and touches everything with shades of pink and gold. At Kilauea, where the road curves to the west, a line of tall, graceful Norfolk pines stands starkly silhouetted against the blazing sky. Even the grasses, their feathery tops waving gently in the evening breeze, are touched with pink, and the cattle grazing in the field seem positioned by an artist's hand. Near Princeville, the clouds, luminous with reflected golds and pinks, seem enormous, dwarfing the cliffs, whose great jagged peaks have turned an astonishing purple.

We never tire of this drive, as each sunset is different—the gleaming expanse of ocean, the sharply angled mountains, the masses of clouds are blended each night by the sun's magic into a composition of colors that will never occur again in exactly the same way. One night the sun's descent may be screened by great masses of clouds rimmed with gold and glowing tangerine against the deep purple mountains and the shimmering blue gray sea. Another time the sun may almost blind you with its blazing, fiery gold, suffusing nearby clouds with impossible shades of orange and pink and brushing distant clouds with peach. Or, one evening the clouds may be so thick that the setting sun is apparent only in delicate touches of apricot on the clouds hovering over the sea, muted purples on the mountains, and the silver sheen on the surface of the sea. As the seasons change, so does the angle of the sun, gilding the landscape with new patterns of light and color.

In fact, as we discovered one summer, a sunset in the rain is the most astonishing of all, for it excites the imagination with impossible combinations. The tops of the mountains are shrouded with gray, yet above the sea, the sky is brilliant with color, with sunny clouds stretching along the horizon, their shapes rimmed with pink light from the setting sun. As dark showers move across the horizon like 'legs of the rain,' blurring the line between ocean and sky, the sun's vivid orange is turning the water purple and the clouds violet. The sun descends into stormy clouds moving slowly toward it, and, as the last light fades, dark clouds hovering above the cliffs slowly creep across the mountains, and the world turns slowly still and dark.

If the clouds are not too thick, there are several places at Hanalei to enjoy the dramatic moment when the shining disk of sun slips silently into the sea. Less than a mile past the entrance to Princeville, you can park at a scenic overlook on Rt 56 and see most of Hanalei Bay's western side. But you have to contend with the distractions of traffic and car radios as well as the conversations of other sunset seekers ("Ralph! I *told* you we were going to miss it! We should have left earlier!") For a more panoramic view with greater privacy, enter Princeville and follow the signs to Pali Ke Kua, park in the lot, and enjoy the view discreetly from the lawn between the buildings.

The drive home after dinner is another sensuous experience of cool evening breezes you can almost taste as well as feel. As you drive south almost alone on the road, you can hear wonderful sounds—the chirping of crickets, the leaves rustling in the breeze— and see the different shades of darkness in the landscape, lit by the moon against an enormous star–filled sky and the shimmering waves of the wide ocean beyond.

The Hanalei Gourmet

For years, on our way to the beach at Hanalei, we have wished for a first rate deli where we could buy sandwiches for picnics on the sand. Now, the Hanalei Gourmet has opened in the old Hanalei schoolhouse, featuring home-baked breads and pastries, wonderful deli meats and salads, fine cheeses, soups, *sashimi* and other *pu pus*, and a selection of gourmet foods and fine wines. Insulated backpacks are available for picnics. Order a wonderful sandwich (about $5) at the deli counter (or phone ahead), or take a table in the 'classroom' next door, converted into an attractive cafe *cum* bar for those who would prefer to avoid the sand altogether! Fans and the large schoolroom windows keep the breezes moving and the temperature comfortable. Afterwards, walk to the Wishing Well for first-rate shave ice.

Across from Ching Young Village Center, Hanalei. Open 8 am to 10 pm daily. 826-2524. Credit cards. Custom picnic baskets. Entertainment 4 nights a week in the bar. Map: 6

Hanalei Shell House

The Shell House has the kind of bar where the bottles provide more than half the decor, with the rest contributed by a Lions Club sign, an antique rifle, and a painting of a mountain scene. And the bar is more than half the decor for the dining room, with the remainder contributed by leafy plants. The small dining room, containing only eight tables, is also perched right on the street. In the days when you could count the number of cars traveling Rt 560 on your fingers, this location was a plus. Now traffic noise is distracting.

Lunch will be expensive for a family. Children have to order adult portions, and sodas are priced as bar beverages at nearly $1 each. The menu features four different burgers, several sandwiches and salads, with the best deal the combination of clam chowder, the Shell House's specialty, and a sandwich for $5.75. The clam chowder ($2.50 for a cup; $3.95 for a bowl) is truly special, made with real cream, delicately flavored with rosemary, and chunky with clams and potatoes. Charbroiled hamburgers ($4.75) are variable, sometimes juicy and tasty though on more than one visit overcooked, even burnt on the outside. If this happens to you, simply send it back for a remake! For the picky eaters in our family, the other sandwiches were even less reliable. Our daughter's *quesadilla* ($5.50) was too mushy and soggy for easy eating. The fresh *ahi* sandwich ($6.95) contained a thin steak, tasty but somewhat dry, accompanied with homemade tartar sauce. Sandwiches include steak fries, baked beans, or cole slaw, and some come with a tasty pasta salad which fortunately our youngest loved, for she ate every available tiny cup. The dinner menu contains many of the same selections, as well as steaks and seafood, priced from $9.95 (hamburger, soup, salad) to $18.95 (cajun blackened fish and salad).

In Hanalei village. Breakfast and lunch daily 8 am- 6 pm daily (Sunday Brunch 8-11:30 am). Dinner from 4:30 pm daily. Map: 6

La Cascata, Princeville Resort Hotel

As soon as you drive up to the Princeville Hotel, you know that arriving is meant to be etched in your memory forever. The entrance faced in marble, opposite a spectacular fountain, sets the scale at impressive. The lobby is enormous, the smooth and shining marble floor seeming like an entry into Alice's wonderland. Along the western wall, enormous windows which appear to be seamless reveal the spectacular colors and contours of the cliffs beyond Hanalei Bay. In this wonderful spot is a beautiful lounge called "The Living Room," where you can sip a glass of wine, or a cocktail, and in the afternoons, enjoy afternoon tea and scones. Comfortable sofas invite you to curl up and look out over Hanalei Bay, glistening in the sunlight as the colors deepen to rich gold and orange. Lovely melodies played by musicians add to the witchery of the moment.

Walk down one level below the Living Room, and you will find La Cascata, with an equally beautiful panoramic view of Hanalei Bay. At sunset, you can watch the sky break in brilliant gold and orange waves across the mountains. The sunset views are more spectacular than the understated decor of the dining room itself, where the soft golden terra cotta color on the walls and quarry tile on the floors create an informal, comfortable ambiance. Tables widely spaced for privacy are set among numerous arches, painted with ivy to resemble an antique garden. Murals provide scenes of Italian landscapes. Candle lamps cast flickering golden light on the tables, covered with white linen, and surrounded with comfortable upholstered armchairs.

Crunchy pizza bread served with a delicious mild pesto spread helps put you in the best frame of mind to consider the menu, which offers ten entrees, as well as an assortment of pastas, appetizers and soups. Minestrone ($5) was filled with crunchy vegetables although the seasoning lacked character. Cream of tomato soup with shrimp and spinach ($6.50) was more distinctive, smooth and delicately flavored. Spinach salad was excellent, as was a salad of green beans, bell peppers, and sauteed quail with chianti vinaigrette ($8.75). Ravioli with ricotta and spinach was perfectly cooked and served with a flavorful butter and sage sauce ($10.50).

Though interesting in conception, entrees are sometimes uneven in execution. Rack of lamb ($26.50) was not particularly tasty, and grilled swordfish ($21.50), accompanied by a delicious eggplant compote, was somewhat dry. Much better was the grilled sirloin steak, perfectly cooked and served with a marinade of olive oil, herbs, sun dried tomatoes and arugula ($24.75). Fresh *ahi* was wonderfully flaky and tender, although served with a sauce far too overpowering for the fish. Veal scallopini ($26.75) was well prepared, though the somewhat heavy wine sauce needs more subtlety. Best of all was fresh seabass, both tender and moist, and served with a gently flavored sauce.

Service is polite, pleasant, and professional. Sommelier Todd Williamson will offer to select wines by the glass to accompany each course of your dinner, or you can choose a bottle from the extensive, and expensive, wine list containing French, German, Italian and Australian wines, as well excellent California choices, like an '89 Sonoma Cutrer Les Pierres vineyard at $47, and an '89 Lageder Pinot Grigio for $37. Our standard of measure, Robert Mondavi Fume Blanc, is fairly priced at $23.

To complete your dinner, try the delicious apple tart $6.50 or an amaretto souffle ($6.50/pp). After dinner, stroll around the hotel, perhaps take a walk down to the beach level and look at the moonlight sparkling on the waves. When planning your dinner, try if possible to set the time for sunset, when the dining experience is gilded with the spectacular colors of sunset.

In the Princeville Hotel. Dinner nightly. Reservations 826-9644. Credit cards. Coffee $2.

Tahiti Nui

If you pull up to Tahiti Nui on some nights, the dining room may be almost empty and you'll think you've come to the wrong place. On another night, however, you might not find a place to put your car. Local people have enjoyed Tahiti Nui for years, since Louise Marston first opened the doors and created its special character as a place where tourists can find the authentic "folk" Kauai. As with most attempts to be folksy, the result is a combination of the genuine and the contrived. Spontaneous entertainment is arranged each night; local musicians drop in from time to time, and guests are told with a twinkle that no one is ever quite sure what is going to happen.

The bar, not the dining room, is the real hub of Tahiti Nui. Decorated in what can only be described as early grass shack, the small, darkened lounge has touches of the genuinely unique (an inflated blowfish used as a lantern) as well as the genuinely corny (the portrait of the topless Tahitian perched over the cash register). The bar is a favorite spot for local people to talk to old friends over generous drinks. For tourists, it's a great place to meet old timers and hear fascinating stories about the island. Even Tahiti Nui's famous 'family style luau' is more like a local talent show than the typical "Hawaiian" extravaganza. Entertainment is provided by Louise's family, as well as whoever happens by, usually local performers on their time off, and occasionally even guests!

On the other nights, Tahiti Nui is like any other restaurant — or almost. Recent remodeling may have made the dining room more attractive and modernized the tiny kitchen, where you used to be able to watch the chef stir and chop and nibble and chat. But Tahiti Nui is still in a class by itself. For what can you say about a place where the carafe of house wine is the most expensive white wine on the menu, if indeed there are any other wines on the menu that night? Where the dinner menu features only six dinners, and one of the choices is squid? Well, expect the unexpected. With an exotic cocktail, you might sample some wonderful crisp won tons ($4.75) served on a bed of lettuce and shredded carrot. Though last year's dozen has shrunk to nine, the won tons have the light crunchiness that only comes from being cooked to order. Jeff, the chef for the last few years, seasons with flair and finesse. Tomato soup ($2) was sensational, served piping hot in a chicken stock rather than cream base, thick with zucchini and tomatoes and garnished with scallions. Won ton soup, by comparison, was a little flat, though colorful with green onions, mushrooms and grated carrot.

Dinners include a small salad, rice, and hot fresh garlic bread. The New York steak, marinated in a subtle *teriyaki* sauce, was crisp yet juicy and exceedingly tender, and a good size considering its modest price ($12.95). An extra bonus, it came with a first-rate baked potato. The fresh *ono* ($16.95) was moist, flaky, and flavored with a delicious butter and wine sauce. Both were accompanied with sauteed zucchini, onions and tomatoes. Your other menu choices are *calamari* ($14.95), chicken curry ($10.95) freshwater prawns ($16.95) and pork ribs ($12.95). Finish off your meal with a slice of excellent macadamia nut pie ($1.75).

Lunch is a gamble at Tahiti Nui. First, the restaurant may or may not be open (Louise closes when business is slow), and even if you're in luck, the kitchen may not have what is on the menu. In fact, the kitchen may not have a chef at all, as happened on our last two tries. This was a great disappointment to our children, sandy and starving and not in the mood for compromise! They wanted the huge turkey sandwiches ($4.75) and the wonderful cooked-to-order hamburgers ($3.75)! They also remembered the serendipity possible in a tiny restaurant, the time when the waitress served our family, which took up two tables, double baskets of hot, buttery garlic bread for the single order price ($1.75), or the time when the chef offered us all some soup, because she was about to cook up a fresh pot and needed to finish off the day's supply first! Because lunch at Tahiti Nui is such a family favorite, we hope Louise gets someone into the kitchen before our next vacation!

In the heart of Hanalei village, on Rt 56. Reservations 826-6277. Luau Wednesday & Friday at 7 pm. Nightly entertainment in Lounge. Credit cards.

Beware the Hawaiian Sun

If you lie out in the sun between 11:30 am and 2:30 pm, you will fry like a pancake, even in a half hour, because Hawaii lies close to the equator and the sun is exceedingly strong. Even on cloudy days, ultraviolet rays can cause a burn. Many sunscreens contain PABA, although this ingredient can give some people a rash. Some of the new 'paba-free' sunscreens are also highly effective. The best lotions protect skin against both UV and UA rays. Choose *'waterproof'* rather than *'water-resistant'* lotions, though don't put too much faith in the manufacturers' claims! Even waterproof sunscreens wash off in salt water and should be re-applied after an hour—or two hours at the most. We've had good results with Johnson and Johnson's Sundown, which forms a skin-like coating that seems good for about two hours, and with sticky gels like 'Bullfrog' and 'Beaver.'

Children need special care and effective lotions. Many dermatologists currently recommend a lotion rated SPF 15, or at least not less than SPF 8. For spots which kids rub often, like right under the eyes, you can try 'Bullfrog' or Chapstick #15. It's a good idea to make a firm rule that kids get "greased up" in the parking lot before heading for the beach as they hate to stand still once the sand is in sight! Bring tee-shirts (the most reliable sun-protection!) for after-swimming sandcastle projects. Schedule family beach visits for the early morning or late afternoon, and plan meals, naps, or drives for the noonday hours. Sunburns are often not visible until it is too late, but you can check your child's skin by pressing it with your finger. If it blanches dramatically, get the child a shirt or consider calling it a day. Keep a spare lotion in the car, for without lotion, it's not worth going to the beach!

Babies need a complete sunblock since their skin lacks the melanin, which produces tanning, until they are about 9 months old. A hat will protect the scalp; use lotion everywhere else, even on feet! Babies should stay in the shade as much as possible– or take an umbrella to the beach!

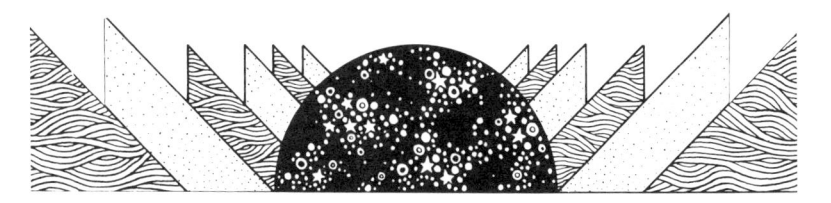

Eastern Shore Restaurants

Al and Don's

There used to be a sign outside boasting 25 breakfast selections. Now it's gone, but no matter. The food never was very good anyway, and the real attraction at Al and Don's is the view. From roomy booths next to enormous windows, you can see the ocean, rimmed with ironwoods, stretching out to the horizon. The decor, though nondescript, is pleasant, and the tables are large and comfortable. Waitresses bring coffee immediately, and your order is prepared quickly and served cheerfully. Food is reasonably priced though not memorable. Pancakes are a trifle heavy, and the corned beef hash, mediocre. Eggs are the best bet.

We had visited Al and Don's only for breakfast, when we could enjoy the restaurant's best attraction—the view! But as an experiment, we sent the four short people for a special outing, dinner by themselves. The results were, in a word, mixed. Only one of our four actually ate what was served, and their observations had the compassion and tact one would expect at their ages: the chicken cutlet was like rubber; the chicken stir fry was cold and mushy; the mashed potatoes were sticky; and jello was the best part of the meal. Their parting recommendation (which might well have been reciprocated by management, judging from our oldest child's description of the deportmenl of our youngest) was "Don't come back." On the other hand, prices are reasonable and, if you time your dinner carefully for before sunset—you might enjoy the view with better luck!

In the Kauai Sands Hotel, at the southern end of the Coconut Plantation Marketplace, Wailua. Credit cards. 822-4951. Open 7 am-10 am, and 6 pm-8:45 pm daily. Map: 5

Barbecue Inn

With a comfortable, attractive, air-conditioned dining room, Barbecue Inn offers one of the best food values on the island. And it's the rare kind of place which will offer something special to just about everyone in the family. Grown-ups will love the shrimp tempura and teriyaki steak combination plate. The tempura is light, crispy and delicate, and the teriyaki steak skewers very tender and tasty. Accompanied by appetizer, soup or salad, homemade bread, vegetable, dessert, and a beverage, this is a real steal for under $10.

Kids will love the cheeseburger ($2.75), which you have to order off the lunch menu even at dinner. Bacon costs 75 cents extra, but it's a small price to pay for a burger which arrives still sizzling on a toasted sesame bun smothered with melted cheese and garnished with fresh, local manoa lettuce! Kids can order fried chicken, hamburger, spaghetti, or chow mein dinners for only $3.75. Grown-ups will love the teriyaki steak ($7.95), a good-sized, tender rib-eye with perfectly flavored homemade sauce, or teriyaki beef kabob and shrimp tempura ($10.95). Fussy eaters can choose from an enormous menu of 25 dinners—fresh fish, seafood platter, T-bone steak, prime rib — from $6.95–$12.95.

You will be surprised at the high quality of the "extras" which many restaurants pay scant attention to. Bread is homemade—light, fragrant, and exceptionally tasty. Your plastic basket will also contain some homemade "lavosh" which is buttery, almost like shortbread. It's so good, you will want seconds, so splurge on an extra order for only 60 cents. The fruit cup appetizer is fresh—pineapple, papaya, watermelon, honeydew, and mango—and so wonderful that you'll hope your kids will refuse to eat theirs because there are no canned peaches! The green salad would win no awards for imagination, but you'd be surprised at how much fun the kids have picking out the shredded cabbage and homemade croutons! And everyone will devour the homemade pies—coconut, chocolate, or chocolate cream—pies so light they are almost as amazing as the price: 75 cents a slice, 10 cents more than a Coke!

You will see a lot of working people coming off the job, and the portions are so enormous you can understand why. Waitresses are unfailingly cheerful, even when small children decorate the floor with crumbs and ice cubes. All this makes Barbecue Inn a good dinner choice for hearty eaters and hungry families, for anyone who appreciates ordinary food cooked extraordinarily well, as well as some very special treats.

In Lihue. 2982 Kress St. (off Rice St.). Closed Sundays. Dinner 4:40 pm-8:45 pm. No credit cards. 245-2921. Map: 4

The Bull Shed

The Bull Shed has been famous on Kauai for years because of its prime rib—a thick slice of tender beef with a tasty bone (if you ask for it) and delicious, fresh horseradish sauce—still reasonably priced at $17.95, though prices have been creeping up dollar by dollar over the past years. Unfortunately, the Bull Shed has also been famous for the long waits due to the no-reservations policy. And don't look for sympathy from the staff—they're used to people standing around and looking unhappy.

We have tried hard to beat the system. We have done our best, despite cranky kids and a frazzled babysitter, to arrive before 7 pm. On one visit, we even collected six friends to qualify for a reservation, but still ended up waiting.

A glance at the menu will tell you why the Bull Shed remains so popular. Entrees come with rice and the salad bar, and half cost less than $15. Combination dinners are served with a 7.5 oz tenderloin filet instead of the usual small sirloin. The wine list is also reasonable, with more than half the selections less than $20, including a Silverado Chardonnay reasonably priced at $19.95. If you choose a white wine, order it right away because your bottle might need time to chill.

The Bull Shed is becoming one of our favorite family restaurants. Our 6:30 pm arrival time is early enough to beat the crowds, and all four children eat everything that is served to them—a rare achievement. Mirah's and Lauren's *teriyaki* chicken breast ($10.95) was perfectly soft and juicy. Mikey was thrilled with the teriyaki sirloin ($13.95), and Jeremy loved his rack of lamb ($16.95), tender and tasty with a delicious *teriyaki* marinade. Even better, all four put away huge and healthy-looking salads, picking their pickiest best from the array of choices on the salad bar.

During our last several visits, service has been efficient and accommodating. Our favorite waitress, Lynn Logan, has watched our children grow taller and hungrier over the years, and our favorite table, just a few feet from the edge of a seawall, offers a spectacular view of the waves rolling towards the wall and crashing in torrents of spray. During a storm, the waves splash right against the glass, an awesome sight! Try to come when the moon is full and watch the waves send gleaming ripples through the darkness. If it's warm, be sure to request a table by a window which opens (not all do). Breezes in this restaurant are hard to come by!

In Kapa'a on Rt 56. Reservations for parties of 6 or more. 822-3791. Credit Cards. Children's menu. Look for the sign (it's small) opposite McDonald's just north of the Coconut Plantation Marketplace, and turn towards the water. Map: 5

Cafe Portofino

You'd hardly expect to find an elegant gourmet Italian restaurant in a shopping center across from the service entrance to the Westin Kauai! But hold onto your hats! Cafe Portofino is really special, with excellent food, attentive service, as well as an exceptionally pretty dining room.

The room is bright, spacious, and cheerful, the white walls accented with honey–colored wood trim and leafy green plants. At night, skylights let in the moonlight. Well–spaced tables are covered in linen and set with shining crystal, and the softly upholstered chairs are absolutely wonderful— they swivel and gently rock, and offer excellent lumbar support. Outside, a terrace offers more informal dining, and at lunch you can catch a glimpse of Kalapaki Bay beyond the Anchor Cove Shopping Center.

Your meal will be both tasty and generous, particularly the fresh, homemade pastas which are simply superb. Feather light *gnocchi* arrive with a delicious sauce of chicken broth flavored with leeks and thickened with potato rather than cream. Flavorful minestrone ($3.25) is served in a huge bowl filled with vegetables crunchy enough to taste separately, in a generous portion for a modest price. Vegetarian lasagne ($10.75) arrives in a huge portion, as festive looking as a wrapped birthday present. It tastes just as wonderful, the flavors and textures of fresh zucchini and spinach brought together with a wonderful marinara sauce with tasty chunks of tomato–a delicious medley of flavors.

We also discovered about the best veal *piccata* ($15.75) on Kauai, carefully grilled to enhance its delicate flavor while keeping it exceedingly tender.   Served piping hot, this elegant dish is colorfully garnished with a large slice of zucchini and peeled fresh tomato. Like the entrees, desserts are generous and beautifully presented, the *profiterolles* ($4.50) exceptionally smooth and filled with delicious custard.

Service is very professional yet friendly, and the seemingly international staff works together with an infectious camaraderie. Everyone seems to care about your dinner, and they're all willing to fetch extra bread or answer questions.

In a location where several restaurants have failed since 1981, Cafe Portofino meets a real need on Kauai for a first-rate Italian restaurant with an elegant setting, reasonable prices, and professional service.

In the Pacific Ocean Plaza, across from Anchor Cove. 245-2121. Credit cards. Closed Sundays. Map: 4

Dani's

At Dani's, you won't find an orchid on your plate, but if you order eggs, what you will find will be hot, tasty, and filling. Toast and kona coffee come free with breakfast, and you can choose from eggs, omelettes, pancakes, and Hawaiian dishes. The ham and cheese omelette is very cheesy and stuffed with ham, though the hotcakes are on the heavy side. Papaya pancakes intrigued us, until we discovered they were an uncommon item for good reason, a soggy consistency. The menu also offers a wide variety of sandwiches and hamburgers as well as lunch plates with salad, and an inexpensive New York steak. Full dinners feature Hawaiian, American, and

Japanese dishes. Prices start at $4.50 and include soup or salad, roll, rice, and coffee or tea.

With prices this low, expect to sacrifice atmosphere. The color scheme is woodgrain formica accented by florescent lights, but on the other hand, the large, modern dining room is bright, clean, and comfortably air-conditioned. Service is swift and efficient, and the hours are convenient for everything but late afternoon snacks and middle of the night cravings.

4201 Rice St. in Lihue, across from Pay 'n Save. Breakfast 5 am-11 am. Lunch 11 am-2 pm. Sunday hours 6 am-11 am. 245-4991. Credit cards. Map: 4

Dragon Inn

Perched on the second floor of a small shopping center on Rt 56 near Kapa'a, Dragon Inn looks big, bright, and cheerful. Inside, the dining room is clean, if sparsely furnished. The decor may be no more than the sum of its parts _ woodgrain formica tables, green leafy plants, and a red carpet, but the windows frame beautiful Sleeping Giant mountain, the tables are not overly close together, and the food is terrific!

This is a first-rate family restaurant. Waiters are very tolerant of the inevitable whining amid the dining. After listening with a smile to our kids describe what they would refuse to eat if he brought it to the table, our waiter politely revised their orders as they worked out the final details of who would share what with whom. He seemed to know that once he got the egg rolls on the table, the cranky crew would settle down, their behavior following that timeless rule: you can't chew and complain at the same time. And he was right. After superb egg rolls ($4 for 3), fried won tons and *gau gee* ($3 each), the main courses proved as generous as the prices are reasonable. As the kids got down to the work of dividing up everything into precisely equal portions, we adults recognized that we had passed that magical point when everyone's plate has something on it and you know the rest of the meal is coasting.

Silver Flower Scallop soup ($4.95) was delicious and piping hot, more popular with the children than chicken and corn soup ($4.50) which had "things" in it. The beef and broccoli ($4.75) was so tasty that the short people clamored for a second platter, which we ordered with noodles. It was even better! Chicken with bamboo shoots and vegetables ($4.75) was full of tender chicken. Cake noodle was crispy and tasty, and served with generous chunks of meat. The shrimp canton ($4.75), with eight juicy shrimp, was a perfect balance of sweet and sour. And when seven can feast for $73 including tip, that's a good deal as well as a good meal.

There is no wine list to speak of, but you can order chardonnay, cabernet, and white zinfandel by the carafe, as well as Chinese beer and all the tea you can hold. Come early for dinner; by the time we left at 7:45, the place was packed! We saw lots of families, some with three generations, and several high chairs. If you try Dragon Inn for lunch, you can order an unbeatably priced lunch special with soup and a choice of 12 entrees for only $3.95.

In the Waipouli Plaza, on Rt 56 in Wailua.
Reservations 822-3788. Take–out menu.
Lunch 11 am - 2 pm.
Dinner 4:30 pm - 9:30 pm. Closed
Sunday and Monday. Map: 5

Duke's Canoe Club

You enter Duke's at beach level and ascend a stone stairway carved into an indoor waterfall draped with ferns and trailing flowers. At the top is a palm-thatched hut with a coconut tree center post where a host appears to escort you to a dining veranda. Cooled by delightful evening breezes, it's a perfect spot to look out over lovely Kalapaki Bay and watch the setting sun tint the clouds with gold.

Duke's offers the same high quality, reasonably priced menu spiced with Polynesian glitz which has made its sister restaurants, Keoki's and Sharky's, so successful. Since Duke's is perched right on the edge of Kalapaki Bay, however, you can be in the real Hawaii as well as the picture postcard variety.

Duke's menu offers lots of choices for reasonable prices, and dinners include a tossed salad with Caesar salad dressing (It comes with tomatoes!) and fresh baked banana-macadamia nut muffins. True to the emphasis on friendly service, the staff will prepare many of the entrees in appetizer portions. You'll be able to choose from several fresh fish entrees ($19-21), including a tasty and generous *teriyaki ahi* in a, both succulent and tender. Though somewhat dry side, the fresh *ulua* was served with a tasty orange and ginger sauce. Hawaiian spiny lobster tail ($18.95) was also fine, and the sirloin steak ($11.95) was tender, generous and so well trimmed that what you could see, you could eat entirely.

The prime rib ($18.95), however, stopped the flow of conversation. Easily more than the 23 ounces listed on the menu, it was so thick that you didn't know where to begin to tackle it. More like a family size roast, it was a significant dining event, and tender as well as juicy, if not quite as tasty as it could have been. One evening, we arrived at 7:30 to find the ribs all gone! According to our waiter, about 30 prime rib dinners are available each night, about 10 % of the total number of dinners served. So if you want the beef, reserve your ribs when you phone to reserve your table!

Everyone in the family will enjoy Duke's. Children have three dinner choices for less than $9, and even if they raid the adult menu, you won't spend very much more. The food is good, service is efficient and friendly, and the view is spectacular. When crowded, however, waiting time can be frustrating. Think twice about going in the rain, however, for you'll miss the best part if they close the shutters!

On Kalapaki Beach, in front of The Westin Kauai. Park at the Westin or at Anchor Cove and walk over. Reservations a day in advance 246-9599. Dinner 5-10 pm daily. Duke's Grill open downstairs 4 pm to midnight for sandwiches, burgers, barbecue plates, ice cream drinks & cocktails. Coffee: $.95. Map: 4

The Eggbert's

Eggbert's dining room is spacious, bright with sunlight, and comfortable. Even better, the kitchen can serve among the finest omelettes on the island. You can choose from 11 varieties, including sour cream and chives ($4.75), fresh mushroom ($4.75), and the "vegetarian delight" ($6.45) which is so stuffed you can hardly get your mouth around it, but be sure to ask the kitchen to hold the onions unless you love them sharp! Larger, 3-egg omelettes are also available for more money (not to mention cholesterol).

No matter the egg count, omelettes are accompanied by rice or hash brown potatoes or toast. Separately priced additions allow you to transform the basic 2-egg omelette ($3.50) into your own creation, and if your omelette comes out on the dry side, be sure to complain, and the staff will cheerfully bring another one. The breakfast menu also features five styles of eggs benedict (from $4.95/half order), delicious banana pancakes ($4.75), and a 'before 9 am' special ($3.85). Children can choose pancakes ($1.65), 'pig in a blanket' ($2.15), or an egg plate ($1.65 and up). Coffee is $.85 and is brought immediately. Service can be on the poky side, so families might want to order some a la carte toast right away.

4483 Rice St. in Lihue. Credit cards. Breakfast/Lunch daily. 7 am-3 pm. Coffee $.85. 245-6325. Map: 4

Hamura Saimin Stand

According to rumor, Oahu businessmen have flown to Kauai just to have lunch at Hamura Saimin. To look at the weather-beaten exterior, you'd have your doubts. The tiny building encloses—just barely—twin rectangular counters with stools. A recent face-lift has made the room look cleaner and more like a luncheonette, but now that the kitchen has been moved out of the center and into the back, you can no longer have a ring-side seat to watch the cook stir and chop and make things sizzle. The inevitability of change, yes, though some traditions die hard. The sign still warns: "No Gum Under the Counter." This year, our kids were old enough to check!

On this counter is served some of the finest *saimin* around, and you come to want to believe the rumor about the Oahu businessmen and their expense account lunches. Airfare could certainly be offset with bargain food prices: for $2.30 you get the *saimin* special—tasty and fragrant soup with noodles, chock full of vegetables and meats. The perfectly flavored won ton soup or won ton min is only $2.60. To take the *saimin* out costs .30 extra for the container, but it's worth it to escape the cramped little room and head for the beach. Barbecued beef or chicken sticks at $.75 are another find, tasty, moist, and perfectly spiced. Light, homemade *manapu* (a sweet cousin of the pretzel) is a great dessert for kids, while adults can try the *lilikoi* chiffon pie ($.95).

There's not much variety, but what the cook cooks is very good indeed, and the visit is like a trip into the island's past, a time before tourism brought butcherblock tables and bentwood chairs, air-conditioning and gourmet teas—a time when sticking gum under the counter, though frowned upon, was still possible. So throw away your Bubble Yum before going inside, and try this taste of authentic Kauai!

2956 Kress St., Lihue. Cash only. 245-3271. Map: 4

Hanama'ulu Restaurant & Tea House

You could not select a better place to share a really special evening with friends than the Tea House, because this restaurant combines delicious food with the friendliest service on the island, and, as if that weren't enough, a Japanese garden setting to make everything seem just a bit magical. Here you can dine on soft mats at low tables next to the goldfish and water lilies. Children can wander around and count the carp (tell them to be careful; one of our two-year-olds tumbled in!). Local families have been coming to the Tea House for more than sixty-five years! Today they still appreciate superb cooking at reasonable prices, and it's a rare wedding, anniversary, welcome or farewell party that does not take place in one of the tea rooms by the garden. So reserve your tea room several days in advance!

The Miyake family cooks with subtlety and flair, and creates a genuinely special cuisine, with 35 Chinese and Japanese entrees at reasonable prices from $3.25-$13.50. We recommend the won ton soup ($4) as the finest anywhere, generously garnished with scallions, pork, and slices of egg foo young. Children will love the crispy fried chicken with its delicate touch of ginger ($4.75); the boneless pieces are just the right size for little hands. Also try crispy fried shrimp ($7.50) and *teriyaki* beef skewers ($5.75).

When our party is large enough, we ask the owner to order a several course dinner. And we are always delighted with the new dishes we discover. The lobster with special butter is superb — exceedingly tender and subtly flavored. Shrimp *tempura* ($8) is spectacular, served on an enormous, beautiful platter, and the taste is just as wonderful. *Sashimi* is fresh and beautifully arranged, the slices of *ahi* and *ono* both slender and fragrant. A specialty, mushrooms stuffed with crab ($5), is lighter than many versions of the dish, and very tasty. In fact, each time we think we have discovered everything wonderful about this restaurant, we are surprised with a new creation, like crispy *tofu tempura* ($3.25) served with *teriyaki* sauce and green onions, or incredibly tasty deep fried scallops wrapped in bacon and served with asparagus. Chinese chicken salad arrived with lots of chicken, lettuce, crispy noodles, and wonderful sauce. A new favorite for Mirah, our vegetarian—the vegetarian spring rolls!

Reserve at least three days in advance to choose where you dine. Avoid the front dining room where service can be rushed and ambiance non-existent. You might prefer the *teppan yaki* room and *sushi* bar. Our favorite, however, is the tea house by the gardens, where we can listen to crickets sing the songs of evening while stars light up the velvet sky. If mosquitoes like to pick on you while ignoring your friends, don't be bashful about asking for a mosquito coil. The incense smell is great, and it keeps the bugs away.

Over ten years of dining here, this special restaurant has never let us down. The cooking is consistently superb, the prices remarkably reasonable, the service exceptionally friendly, and children are treated with more than usual tolerance by waitresses like Sally and Arlene who genuinely love them. Because this is a restaurant where you should sample as many dishes as possible, and because it is such a special place, we like to save the Tea House for our last night with our Kauai friends, and ask any *kapunas* who might be listening to speed our return! You shouldn't miss the Tea House either.

Call Sally for reservations or to arrange special dinner menus at 245-2511. Avoid the front dining room. Credit cards. Full bar. House wine: Robert Mondavi ($6/$10). Closed Mondays. Lunch 9 am-1:30 pm; Dinner 4:30 pm-9:30 pm. Banquet facilities. Map: 4

Inn on the Cliffs, Westin Kauai

As you should expect at the Westin, your meal is only the main course of your evening, which begins ceremoniously with a ride aboard an elegant Venetian launch on a romantic journey across an enormous man-made lagoon, where fountains splash in shining arcs through statues of fanciful beasts and fish. Come at sunset, when the sky turns brilliant with reds and oranges.

The restaurant's elegant three-level design takes full advantage of its cliff-side perch on the edge of Kalapaki Bay. You enter at the middle level, and as you stand in the foyer, suspended between the lounge upstairs behind you and the dining level in front of you below, you look out to sea through giant windows. Open to all three stories, the dining room has the sense of great space and light, and yet despite its grand dimensions, which may remind you at once of a baronial castle or an art museum, the room has an almost contradictory feeling of intimacy. Each table, with its cluster of plushly upholstered chairs, seems to create its own separate space, and the Oriental carpets and fine works of art can make you feel as if you're dining in a private home. White linen cloths are set with gleaming china and silver, fresh orchids bloom in white seashells, and candles twinkle in brandy glasses. In the bar upstairs you'll even find a fireplace for damp rainy nights, with two couches just the right size for close encounters.

Dinner could not be more relaxing. Melodies from the piano seem to rise, then float down to the lower levels. Through the giant windows, you can watch the waves roll slowly into the bay, crested with white foam and gleaming in the moonlight. Or, because the restaurant is also in the glide path for the airport, you can watch the jets, headlights ablaze in the night sky, fly past the restaurant's huge windows to bring the next load of lucky vacationers to the garden isle.

But the view and the restaurant, spectacular as they are, make up only part of Inn on the Cliffs's special charm. The fresh seafood is wonderful, and even though the original chef recently left to teach courses at Kauai's Community College, his recipes and high standards still reign in the kitchen. You'll find a lot to choose from on the menu. In addition to jet-set clams, shrimps, lobster, and oysters, you'll find at least half a dozen local fresh fish ($23-$32), while those who prefer the turf to the surf can choose a first-rate filet of beef ($26) or teriyaki chicken ($16), the least expensive entree.

The specialty of the house is the fresh fish, served in generous portions which can be either broiled or pan fried. The fish is beautifully prepared and attractively served, crispy gold on the outside and yet meltingly tender, with the natural flavors enhanced simply with lemon and butter. Although the kitchen can whip up a delicious herb wine sauce on request, purists like ourselves who love the natural flavors undisguised will appreciate the kitchen's clean, crisp pan frying as the best way to taste the subtle flavors of *onaga* ($27), *ono* ($27), or *mahi mahi* ($27) and *opakapaka* ($29) which pleased a skeptical, first-time fish eater. The chef usually offers at least one special preparation each night, and the sea bass served with straw mushrooms, *tofu*, and *beurre blanc* sauce was firm and soft, with a texture like lobster.

You can choose from a wide array of appetizers, including fresh pastas. Linguini and veal *marsala* ($9.25) is outstanding, as is the linguini ordered "low cholesterol" with only olive oil and garlic. Equally good are the broiled scallops ($8.75), perfectly tender and served with avocado and a delicious salsa with character. Also fine though not quite as special are sauteed ginger shrimp with cilantro and spring onions ($8.50). A less expensive alternative, clam chowder ($4.25) is tasty, creamy and filled with clams.

Service is friendly, professional, and generous in spirit. When our spinach and cheese ravioli with scallops ($8.75) seemed overly salty, our server insisted on making the dish afresh and, in the meantime, brought a complimentary bowl of tasty cream of mushroom soup. The new serving of pasta was perfectly seasoned.

Entrees are served with fresh vegetables, in our case sauteed snow peas, red peppers, and red potatoes garnished with dill. Mini *baguettes* of sweet french bread are warm and tasty, and you'll find excellent light pastries for dessert, like a spectacular hazelnut and chocolate sponge cake.

Unfortunately, the wine list, which was once nearly as outstanding as the fresh fish, has been replaced with the more limited Westin corporate list, but you'll still find some good choices, like a 1988 Sonoma Cutrer, Cutrer Vineyards chardonnay for $34.

The Inn on the Cliffs offers a winning combination: spectacular location, beautiful dining room, friendly service, and delicious fresh seafood. You can't ask for much more, even if prices are higher than in other island seafood restaurants. This is a restaurant you should not miss!

In the Westin Kauai. Reserve at least two days in advance; two seatings, at 6 pm or 8 pm. 245-5050. Free valet parking. Map: 4

Jacaranda Terrace, Kauai Hilton

Arranged on two levels, Jacaranda's attractive dining room looks out over the garden through glass doors that slide open to evening breezes. When weather is not so cooperative, the dining room is closed and comfortably air-conditioned. The upper tier is centered around a large table which offers moderately priced breakfast and dinner buffets. Along the rear wall, tables are recessed for privacy, and you can dine in what seems to be a small private room, tastefully decorated with wallpaper and prints. The result is quiet, relaxing, and very pleasant.

Because most hotel guests eat at this dining room, you can order almost anything—eggs, soup, sandwiches, salads, or hamburgers—at almost any time of day. At dinner, you can also select from 9 entrees served with potato or rice and vegetables. Prices vary widely, from a bowl of saimin to veal marsala, with chicken, shrimp, steak and fish in between. The reasonably priced wine list has several good choices for less than $20.

We began our dinner with soup, a fresh *baguette* and butter. Though expensive for a small cup, the tomato soup was excellent—fresh, pungent with spices, and piping hot, while the cream of *mahi mahi* was rather pasty. Of the entrees, the roast prime rib was the better choice, for it was a good-sized portion, tender, juicy and very tasty. The veal *marsala* would have been better without the thick and heavy sauce which pretty well obliterated the flavor of the veal. Both entrees were served with zucchini and carrots still crunchy and colorful. The baked potato was first rate, served with tiny dishes of sour cream, chives, and crisp bacon. Ordering from the menu seemed a better choice than the buffet, judging from the plates we saw carried by, heaped high with salad, fruit, and entrees with a lot of sauce.

Service is efficient, polite, and very friendly. Such capable staff can make a hotel restaurant into one you may remember even after you pay your bill and are on your way to the airport. If you order carefully, you probably won't have a bad dinner at Jacaranda, and the odds are good that you'll enjoy the evening.

In the Kauai Hilton. Reservations 245-1955. Credit Cards. Children's menu: half price of most selections. Coffee/brewed decaf $1.35 (decaf $1.50 at dinner). Map: 4

Jimmy's Grill

Until a couple of years ago, a ramshackle building dozed on a dusty corner of main street, Kapa'a. Downstairs was home to a few dimly lit stores with wares probably just as well left in shadow, and a bar with the hapless name Ding's. Upstairs, the windows of empty apartments stared down like vacant eyes on the bewildering pace of modern–day doings. Occasionally, the building came briefly to life—on hot fourth of Julys when sales of firecrackers kindled, or when local boxing matches drew the competitive and the curious. Now the weatherbeaten string of sleepy small businesses has been transformed into smart shops featuring upscale memorabilia, as well as a trendy new bar *cum* restaurant called Jimmy's Grill. The "Historic Hee Fat Building" has been reborn!

Jimmy's sign claims "Lunch Forever," and the decor tries to capture the carefree quality of endless waves and suntans. You enter Jimmy's through what used to be Ding's, only now the bar is a full two-story affair completely open to the street on the two sides of its corner location. Once inside, you'll find yourself on an indoor sand dune, improbably set with tables, chairs and an upholstered furnishing labeled "Party Couch." Behind the dune is a wide flight of stairs to the restaurant above, offering those who ascend an ever-changing perspective on a neon topless female winking from her perch on the rear wall. You will also pass by color photos and surfboards marked with the signatures, initials, and greetings of hundreds of happy campers.

The dining room, which takes up the whole top floor of Hee Fat, is pleasantly spacious. White walls and rafters are decorated with colorful surfboards and maritime flags, as well as an occasional pair of sneakers, and banks of green plants separate tables into clusters. Tables for two line the small balcony overlooking the main street of Kapa'a, and on the opposite wall are several roomy booths with bright red vinyl bench seats, the kind that will remind you of stationwagons called woodies. When breezes cooperate, the room is cooled by the cross ventilation, though the booths get some of the smoky smell from the grill, and the balcony gets the exhaust from street traffic. When temperatures climb on main street, however, remember what happens to hot air!

The menu offers burgers, sandwiches, munchies, as well as assorted entrees. We found the food competently prepared if uninspired. Half-pound hamburgers (from $6.50 with fries) are tasty. Nachos ($6.95) had more beans than cheese, and were served with a salsa dominated by red onions. The skinless, all-beef hot dog ($4.50) was large and soft. Voted best by the children: the milk shakes ($2.25), the teriyaki beef sticks ($5) and the 'loaded' potato skins ($6). While lunch, according to the sign, is 'forever,' a dinner menu offers more than a dozen steak, seafood, chicken, and barbecue entrees, priced from $12.95 (chicken) to $18.95 (grilled rib eye steak), including salad, potato or rice, and bread.

You probably won't leave Jimmy's Grill disappointed. The food is adequate, and many people like the friendly openness and laid-back informality. Except perhaps the ghost of Hee Fat, wandering back for one last bewildered glimpse as the sun sets over the mountains.

Main St, Kapaa. 822-7000. Credit cards. Coffee: $.75. Map: 5

JJ's Broiler

Twenty-five years ago, Kauai's first steak house opened in a refurbished plantation house on the main street of Lihue, then a sleepy town with a single traffic light. Named JJ's after its owner, the restaurant achieved local fame for its specialty, "Slavonic steak", a sliced London Broil marinated in a sauce heavily flavored with garlic. When anyone in JJ's was served this dish, everyone else knew it!

All that began to change five years ago, when the Westin Kauai 'megaresort' inaugurated a new age in Kauai's tourism. Deciding it was time to meet the changing times, JJ's owners built a new restaurant right on Kalapaki Bay to challenge the Westin on its own beach with a steak and seafood menu at reasonable prices.

The multi-level design of the new JJ's affords each table some privacy as well as a sweeping ocean view. All that is great, but once you look up, you see an enormous empty space decorated primarily with steel girders. The dining room ends up with the hollow sound of what could be described as industrial open space, and all the warmth and intimacy of an airplane hanger.

Those who liked the old JJ's menu will find few surprises. The star performers are still the steaks, like a 14 oz New York steak ($18.95) which is lean, moist, and tasty. Chicken breast teriyaki is tender enough, and of good size, though the sauce which coated it seemed more an afterthought than part of the design. Most disappointing was the prime rib, which was small, tough, and tasteless, and at $19.95, the same price as Duke's larger portion and $2 more than the outstanding prime rib at the Bull Shed in Wailua.

Dinner begins with sourdough bread and soup. The salad is the major event of the evening, for what arrives at the table is actually a portable salad bar, a huge bowl surrounded by vegetables and condiments in lazy susan. It's a good distraction from the rather undistinguished bread, or a beef and vegetable soup which seems designed to please by being inoffensive.

The new JJ's is definitely a step up from the old, though some will miss the aroma of slavonic steak, which is dissipated by all the open space above. It's no bargain, however. For pretty much the same prices, JJ's faces stiff competition from Duke's just down the beach, where, in our opinion, portions are larger, the food tastier, and the service more skillful.

In Anchor Cove, Nawiliwili. Lunch & Dinner, 11 am-10 pm, daily. Credit cards. Reservations 246-4422. Map: 4

Kapa'a Fish & Chowder House

One of the few seafood specialty restaurants on the eastern shore, the Kapa'a Fish and Chowder House has an attractive exterior decorated with fishing nets and nautical gear. The "garden room" in the rear is a peaceful oasis filled with hanging ferns and plants. Be sure to request it when you make your reservation.

The specialty is fresh seafood, from both local and distant seas. You'll find San Francisco crab, New England bluepoint oysters and steamer clams, sea scallops and Ipswich clams, and shrimps of all kinds. In addition to more than a dozen seafood entrees, the menu offers chicken ($9.95), a 16 oz New York steak ($17.95) and 18 oz of prime rib ($17.95). Entrees include choice of french fries, pasta, rice pilaf or steamed rice, as well as a vegetable, corn fritters and pumpkin muffins. The wine list is limited though reasonably priced, with Soave Bolla listed fairly at $12.50.

During our visits over the years, we have found the cooking to be inconsistent. Sometimes the seafood chowders are excellent, and at other times, overly thick and heavily flavored with thyme. On some visits, the fish has been moist and tender, while at other times it has been overcooked and dry. As a rule, we ask to have the fish broiled or plainly sauteed, so that the filet does not arrive smothered in a heavy wine sauce with capers which overwhelms its delicate flavor. On our last visit, the *opakapaka* ($19) was wonderfully moist and much tastier without the thick sauce which we had wisely ordered confined to a side dish. The *ahi teriyaki* ($18), a generous portion cleanly broiled and very tender, was paired more successfully with its tasty marinade. With the entrees, you get a choice between pasta, which is rather garlicky, or rice, or crisp, hot french fries. The fresh steamed carrots were good though not exceptional. We'd love to try the prime rib, but on our last two visits, none was available when we arrived at 7:30 pm. The top sirloin was a poor second choice, both dry and tough.

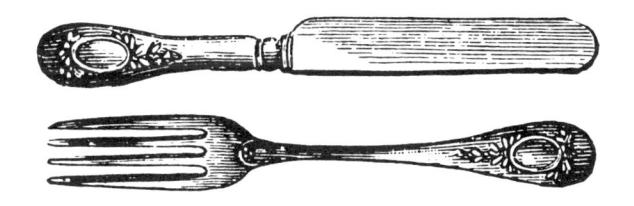

Over the years, service has been uneven—usually well-meaning, but somewhat inept. On one visit, our waiter attempted to insert the corkscrew into the wine bottle without first removing the covering from the cork. More recently, our waiter brought the wrong wine and then, correcting that mistake, broke the cork while opening the right one. On our most recent visit, however, we had the most competent waitress imaginable.

Given the unevenness of the kitchen and the unpredictability of the serving staff, dining at the Kapa'a Fish and Chowder House means taking your chances. If you catch it right, you can enjoy a pleasant seafood dinner in the garden room, softly lit with lanterns and candles. But you'll spend nearly $20 for that dinner, nearly twice what it would cost at the Wailua Marina, for example, where the setting may be less attractive but the fish more reliable.

In northern Kapa'a on Rt 56. Credit cards. Dinner from 5:30 pm daily. Reservations 822-7488. Specify the garden room. Coffee: $.90. Seven children's entrees available at half-price. Map: 5

Kauai Chop Suey

Kauai Chop Suey combines unpretentious surroundings, superb cooking, and unbeatable prices. The dining room, usually crowded with local families, is clean, bright, and cheerful, with well-spaced tables and fly fans to keep the air moving. The decor is a crisp combination of red and white, accented with red Chinese lanterns and green leafy plants.

The real attraction is the prices. A big tureen of scallop soup ($6.05) was sensational, with a subtly seasoned light broth, tender slices of pork and scallops, and an egg-drop texture. The shrimp canton ($5.65) was a perfect balance of sweet and sour, and the shrimps, eight large ones, were still crisp from being deep fried and exceedingly tender. Special fried rice (at $6.50 one of the most expensive dishes on the large menu) was indeed special—especially tasty, especially generous, and chock full of delicious roast pork, chicken, shrimp, black mushrooms and crunchy snow peas. In Kauai Chow Mein ($6.95), shrimp, chicken, steak, and *char sieu* are blended in a colorful combination with broccoli and carrots.

Your level of satisfaction, we discovered, has a lot to do with the service, which has a lot to do with the work load in the kitchen.

Even if you see empty tables, the owner may tell you to come back in 15 minutes, and in this way control the pace at which the three chefs have to cook. Once you are seated, you may not see your waitress for a while. That's because, as we saw on our last visit, there was only one waitress, and she was taking orders from all the tables, while two other waitresses served and a couple of busboys cleared the plates. It's not a very efficient system, and it certainly lacks the personal touch, but the prices are amazing, and you can bring along your own wine or beer to make the waiting more pleasant! Think twice, however, about bringing the kids— unless you feed them before you come! To bring food home will cost you 21 cents a box: you pay and you pack! Be warned: your feet must be across the threshold by 9 pm or you will be told, with great politeness, that the kitchen is closed.

In the Pacific Ocean Center, Lihue. No reservations. Take out 245-8790. Lunch 11-2 pm Tues through Sat. Dinner 4:30-9 pm Tues through Sun. No beer or wine, but tea is free. Map: 4

Restaurant Kiibo & Sushi Bar

Kiibo has a pleasant, though small dining room with a clean, though utilitarian decor. Comfortable upholstered chairs surround bamboo colored tables, and brown lattice adorns the white walls. Everything is understated, even the air-conditioning!

The menu is actually a photo album of traditional Japanese dishes. You can order tempura *a la carte* ($1/selection) and select from five different types of fresh fish, chicken, pork, beans, tofu, onion, sweet potato, carrots, even eggplant. Whatever you choose will be both light and crisp, each flavor unique and meltingly delicious. Even the parsley was crunchy and still green. The *teriyaki* ($5.50) was another success, sweet yet tangy and both juicy and tender. The *sukiyaki* ($6.50) arrived in a steaming iron caldron, rich and pungent with sauce and translucent noodles.

Priced from $4.75, dinners include *miso* soup, a bowl of rice and another of sauce, attractively displayed on a square tray. Combination dinners cost more, between $11 and $15. Lunch is a better deal, however, with selections from $3.85 and about a dollar less than the same choices on the dinner menu. Lunch is also the better meal; given the cautious size of the portions, dinner might leave you hungry! If you spend a little bit more, you could find a better quality dinner in more pleasant surroundings—for example, at Hanama'ulu Restaurant and Tea House, or Kintaro in Kapa'a.

2991 Umi St, Lihue. 245-2560. Cash only! Lunch daily 11 am-1:30 pm. Dinner daily 5:30 pm-9 pm. Closed Sundays & holidays. Children's dinners $5. Map: 4

The King and I

The King and I is one of those wonderful restaurants you always dream of discovering tucked away in a shopping center, like your child's favorite toy under the socks in the corner of his closet. Well, The King and I really is a dream come true, not only for the diner, but also for the owners, a family who fled Cambodia by boat, settled in Hawaii and trained in Honolulu's famous Keo's restaurant, waiting and saving for the chance to open up on their own.

Surprisingly pleasant and comfortably air-conditioned, the dining room is as modest as the prices. White linen tablecloths are topped with glass in an attractive compromise between attractiveness and utility. A definite step above formica! On walls painted a warm and friendly shade of pink are large paintings of Siamese ladies and rural scenes. Orchids and palm leaves give the tables a tropical touch.

But the real attraction at The King and I is the food. For most people, each dish will be an adventure into unknown and exotic tastes. Don't be bashful! The menu is large enough to appeal to a variety of tastes. Everyone will love the spring rolls ($5.95/6) which are crisp and light and wonderfully tasty. Attractively arranged on manoa lettuce with mint leaf and cucumber, and served with a delicious peanut vinegar dipping sauce, the spring rolls are so special that some customers make a meal of several orders!

But it would be a mistake to miss the other dishes that come out of this extraordinary kitchen. Lemon grass soup ($6.95) is served piping hot, with wonderfully fragrant clouds of steam. Shrimps served with a peanut sauce are meltingly tender, attractively arranged with shredded cabbage and tomato wedges. Or try the fried rice ($5.95) flavored with tomato, cucumber, and cilantro and garnished with sliced water chestnuts. Don't pass up the Siam *Mee Kaob* ($4.95), a small mountain of crispy rice noodles, bean sprouts, and scallions, served with a delicately sweet peanut sauce. *Sa-teh,* served with spicy peanut sauce and cucumber dipping sauce, is delicious, whether beef, chicken or the truly amazing fresh *mahi mahi*, light and crisp as a whisper.

Fresh *mahi mahi* is also available as 'Ginger fish' ($8.50), fried crisp and served with a mild sauce flavored with ginger and scallions. Curries are outstanding, and you can select from three. Yellow curry is served with potatoes and onions; flavored with saffron, it would be the easiest to identify as a "curry." The green curry takes its color—and flavor—from fresh basil, as well as coconut, lime leaves,and lemongrass. The red curry was the sweetest, flavored with coconut. Best of all, in our opinion, is a curry not on the menu, but the favorite of a Kauai friend—a mild, sweet curry, flavored with peanut and coconut and chock full of tender chicken. You can ask for it as Evil Jungle Prince ($5.50). Don't miss Siam eggplant ($5.95), pungent and wonderful.

The basil and other spices are grown fresh in Kilauea. Try the special Thai tapioca pudding, which will be more soupy perhaps than the lumpy stuff you may remember from school lunches, and flavored with delicious apple-bananas and coconut. The wine list is modest in both size and price. Most wines cost below $20, as well as beers, including a Thai beer, Singha, in a large bottle for $2.75.

The King and I is a special place, a great choice for those evenings when you find it hard to look at another *ahi* or *ono*. You'll love the change of pace, the distinctive cuisine, and the friendly family atmosphere. And when you get your bill, your royal pocketbook will hardly notice.

4-901 Kuhio Highway, Wailua.
 Reservations two days in advance
822-1642. Map: 5

Gaylord's at Kilohana

Kilohana, once the heart of a 1,700 acre sugar plantation, is a special place. Wandering through rooms which have the spacious beauty of large proportions and wide verandas, you can easily imagine the gracious pace of life before airplanes and traffic lights. With the mountains behind and rolling lawns all around, you can glimpse, even if briefly, a way of life now forever lost. Browsing the shops brings you quickly up to date: trendy clothes and jewelry, and in the Kilohana Gallery, a fine collection of work by artists from Kauai and the other Hawaiian islands.

Named for Gaylord Wilcox who built Kilohana, the restaurant is in the dining room and on the veranda, looking out over the manicured lawn and gardens lush with leafy ferns and brilliant tropical flowers. In the evening, the flagstone terrace is lit with lanterns, and rattan chairs surround comfortable tables decked with white linen and pink napkins arranged like fans. Gaylord's is one of the most romantic restaurants on Kauai, with the kind of setting you'd want to star in if your life were a black and white movie. Candles on the tables flicker softly in gentle breezes, and from your chair beneath the roof you can peek out at stars shining in the velvet sky. As you look out at the gardens lit by the moon and stars, you can feel the soft tropical breezes which rustle the leaves. Waiters in tuxedo shirts and cummerbunds move discreetly, anticipating your every desire.

Entrees are expensive, and unless you come for "light supper" (5 to 6:30 pm) your least expensive dinner choice is prime rib, at $18.95. With soup or salad not included in the price of the dinner, the cost of dining goes up quickly. Some choices, however, are extremely reasonable in price, like baked *brie* in *filo,* an enormous portion for a modest $5.95, deliciously creamy and mild.

Over the years of our visits to Gaylord's, we have found the dining experience variable. Sometimes the appetizers are the best part of the meal while the entrees are disappointing. Gaylord's menu shows a preference for elaborate preparations and ingenious sauces, an approach which is sometimes successful, as in sliced duck salad ($4.95), the lean, crispy duck served with a raspberry vinaigrette both sweet and tart, or the rack of lamb ($21.95) served in tender medallions flavored with raspberry and mango. At other times, however, this presentation seems overly elaborate, as in Rainbow duck with three sauces ($19.95),where the flavors quickly mingle and become indistinguishable. Rather than a delicate mix of spices, the blackened *ono* has been simply hot, nearly too hot to handle! While you are encouraged to devise your own combination dinners, your selections can conceivably occupy the same plate without being complementary in flavor or texture. Fresh *ahi* and venison ($29.95), for example, each served with its own special sauce, were like friends who aren't on speaking terms. Prime rib ($18.95), on the other hand, is a good bet, served plainly in a generous portion with lots of *au jus*. Entrees arrive with a vegetable, as well as rice, pasta, or potato. Vegetables—celery, carrots, and cauliflower—are crisp and attractive. Whole wheat rolls are warm and tasty.

Gaylord's wines are expensive. The list includes some excellent California vintners like Chalone and Chateau Montelena, but at sky-high prices, with the low end marked by Round Hill Chardonnay at $18.

Despite the occasional disappointments, the dining experience can still be wonderful. Waiters are polite, attentive, and professional, and in the quiet courtyard, you escape the usual noisy distractions of clattering trays and banging dishes. Small details get lots of attention: water is served in elegant iced glasses with tangy lemon slices, and coffee cups are watched carefully. If you like to linger after dinner, you might want to bring a sweater, for temperatures can be chilly during winter months.

With such an elegant setting, Gaylord's could develop into one of the island's truly special dining experiences, an image to haunt you when temperatures plunge back home. At this point, our feeling is to order as simply as possible. While we have found our dinners to be of uneven quality, however, we have heard high praise of Gaylord's lunch, where excellent sandwiches, salads, vegetable platters and fresh seafood are reasonably priced ($6.95-$10) and you can look out at the garden in the full splendor of Hawaiian sunshine.

Lunch 11 am-4 pm. Dinner 5-10 pm daily. Light Supper 5-6:30 pm. with entrees from $12.95 with salad, rice, & vegetables. Children (under 10) full dinners ($9.95), usually beef, chicken, or fish. Children's full lunches ($3.75) including PBJ and grilled cheese. Sunday brunch 10 am-3 pm. Coffee: $1.00. Gaylord's will dispatch its free limousine or van for special occasions. Map: 4

Kintaro

Walking into Kintaro is like entering a different world. The decor is serene and elegant, a tasteful harmony of blues, whites, grays and tans in perfect proportion. A fountain set in blue tiles and a *sushi* bar displaying a beautiful array of *sashimi* take up one long white wall. On nut-colored wood tables, set with chopsticks in blue and white wrappers, you'll find blue and tan tea bowls, and a striking single flower. Ceiling fans and air conditioning make Kintaro comfortably cool, and subdued Japanese music sets a relaxed mood. The total effect is bright, crisp, and immaculate.

What you choose to eat determines where you sit! If you want cocktails and *pu pus*, you can relax in a comfortable, attractive lounge, beautifully decorated in grays, light woods, and whites. You can sip a wonderful chi chi, sample elegant *sashimi*, or munch on crispy fried won tons from the owner's factory next door, and hot, tasty dumplings. You could almost make a meal of such treats!

In the same spacious room, you can try *teppan yaki* at specially designed tables and watch talented chefs chop and flip and make things sizzle right before your eyes. If you prefer the regular menu, you might be seated in the smaller, more intimate dining room.

No matter where you sit, your food will be delicious, attractive, and presented with impeccable attention to visual detail. Dinners include soup, rice, and sometimes a delicious seafood salad. Each meal is served with great politeness at a leisurely pace, from the first course, a salad of octopus and white cucumbers, to the house dessert, green tea ice cream.

Following a subtle and delicious *miso* soup, dinner entrees are presented on traditional sectioned wooden platforms and include rice, *zaru soba* (chilled buckwheat noodles with a special sauce) and pickled vegetables, along with tea served in a blue and tan pottery teapot. The intent is to present the diner with a sampling of varied tastes, with portions just the right size to tempt and satisfy rather than overwhelm the palate.

Kintaro is one of those rare restaurants that surprise you with each visit. The foods are so fresh and the preparation so subtle that you can confidently put your dinner in the hands of the owner and simply marvel at what he brings to the table. A *sashimi* platter arrived with six elegantly arranged selections, priced at $2.50 each: thin slices of *ahi*, translucent slivers of *ono* which were delicately sweet and fragrant, dark strips of pungent smoked salmon, shrimps cooked so perfectly that they seemed to melt as you tasted them, eel astonishingly sweet and tender. Garnished with pickled ginger, this was a sensational palette of tastes assembled with an eye for beauty as well as a taste for harmonies and contrasts.

During a recent visit, we tried the *teppan yaki* room, and watched the chef, in a dazzling display with twin shining steel spatulas, flip and scoot filets and vegetables across his sizzling grill. The ingredients, as you will see when they are presented to you in their raw form, are fresh and of the best quality. The *teriyaki* New York steak ($18.95) is tender, tasty and juicy. The lobster tail is excellent. The oysters lightly breaded and sauteed in olive oil ($13.95) are plump and tasty.

You won't be disappointed with the selections on the regular menu. Crispy shrimp *tempura* with vegetables ($13.25), for example, is feather light and delicious, particularly the green beans! *Teriyaki* beef made with slices of NY steak is exceptionally tender ($14.95). The beef *sukiyaki* in a cast iron pot ($14.75) is dark and dusky with translucent noodles, meat, and vegetables. Or try *yose nabe* ($11.50), a Japanese *bouillabaisse* generous with seafood, vegetables, mushrooms, and yam noodles in a delicious broth. On one occasion, a fresh water trout, which friends had brought to the restaurant, was prepared with such finesse by the owner that every nose turned as he carried it to our table. While the green tea ice cream may please some but not others, a refreshing choice to complete the meal is Midori honeydew melon liqueur, served either in a slender glass with a slice of lemon, or over ice cream. After dinner you can browse in the adjacent gift shop, which displays Japanese art, jewelry, and porcelains. Children are welcome, as is appropriate for a restaurant named in honor of a legendary Japanese boy hero, and everything seems arranged to be courteous, pleasant, and welcoming. For diners of any age, Kintaro is a must if you are looking for delicious Japanese food in an elegant, comfortable setting.

On Rt 56 in Wailua. House wine: Taylor California Cellars ($6.50). 5:30-9:30 pm daily. Reservations 822-3341. Credit Cards. Map: 5

Kountry Kitchen

For years, and despite changes in ownership, the best spot for breakfast on the island's east coast has been the Kountry Kitchen, which serves terrific food at equally terrific prices. The large menu offers delicious eggs, expertly cooked bacon and sausage, as well as several omelette creations, including sour cream, bacon and tomato ($5.30) and vegetable garden ($6.20). You can even design your own omelette by ordering a combination of separately priced fillings. Kountry Kitchen's omelettes are unique—thin pancakes of egg rolled around fillings almost like a crepe—tender, moist, delicious. Our children usually choose Cheesy Eggs—toasted English muffin topped with bacon and poached eggs and covered with rich, golden cheese sauce ($5.25), and our babies have all loved the honey and wheat pancakes ($2.95), which are light and fragrant even when drowning in a small ocean of syrup. Hash browns are outstanding, perfectly golden and crisp pancakes of shredded potatoes, and portions are generous. Kids love hot chocolate ($.95).

This very popular restaurant gets crowded at peak mealtimes; so plan to arrive a little early because tables get taken up very quickly, mostly by regular customers. The waitresses are pleasant and efficient and pour lots of absolutely delicious coffee. Across the street is a park with a sandy beach for walking afterwards.

The dinner menu features more than a dozen reasonably priced complete dinners, as well as five choices for children. Breakfast beverages include gourmet teas; at lunch or dinner you can order beer and wine. Go early to breakfast—the line is out the door by 8 am!

1485 Kuhio Hwy, just south of Kapa'a. 822-3511. Credit cards. Breakfast 6 am-9 pm daily. Coffee with cream $.95. Map: 5

Kukui Nut Tree Inn

Air-conditioned, bright, and cheerful, the Kukui Nut Tree Inn looks more like California than Kauai. Bentwood chairs surround woodgrain tables, and lots of hanging and potted plants help to create a summer garden. The staff is as pleasant as the setting, and particularly helpful with small children. Our waitress complied readily with one child's request for a straw to go with her cup of cocoa and brought plenty of extra napkins at the same time. For breakfast, the ham and cheese omelette was generous and tasty, and the pancakes pleased our youngest expert. The mushrooms in the omelette were fresh, and the coffee delicious.

Lunch is the busiest time because Kukui Nut Tree Inn attracts the business lunch crowd as well as exhausted shoppers. *Kapunas* (senior citizens) as well as *keikis* (children) have specially priced entrees which include soup or fruit cup; rice or potatoes; beverage, and dessert. The lunch menu is enormous, with 19 sandwiches, 23 lunch entrees (served either a la carte or for $2 more complete with soup) as well as salads and a generous bowl of saimin ($3.75). The kitchen's performance varies widely, and in the case of *teriyaki* beef, quality varies almost from slice to slice, with some tender and others intolerably fatty. *Tempura* ($5.95) was mushy, and the hot roast beef sandwich ($4.50) tough and tasteless. The bright spots were french fries and fried chicken, deliciously tender, hot, and crisp, as well as a generous and tasty club sandwich ($3.50). Don't miss the house special salad dressing made from papaya seeds, with a delicious sweet and spicy taste. Buy some to take home. Although the food is not imaginative or distinctive, Kukui Nut Tree Inn is inexpensive and friendly. And after a hard morning of shopping, that may be all you need.

Kukui Grove Center, Lihue. Open daily for breakfast, lunch, and dinner except Sunday evenings. Credit cards. 245-7005. Map: 4

Makai

The only restaurant on Kauai featuring Mediterranean cuisine, Makai is perched right over the main street of Kapa'a. Despite the drawbacks of the location, the dining room is attractive, with leafy green plants and colorful painted fish dangling from the rafters. Blue and white striped cloths cover the tables—fewer than a dozen—protected by glass tops. Makai serves breakfast, lunch, and dinner, and features such specialty items as *moussaka*, *gyros*, and *shish kebab* as well as Mediterranean dips with *pita* bread.

Prices are reasonable, and so is quality. Complete dinners include bread and rice or vegetables, as well as a choice of salad or soup. Cream of tomato was nicely seasoned though the heap of cold parmesan cheese on top, which stayed in a lump despite efforts to stir, made for some sharp tasting spoonfuls. The dinner salad is of fair size, the creamy *feta* house dressing a welcome change from standard choices. So are the Mediterranean dips ($3.50-$6.95), though a single *pita* bread (additional ones cost extra) may not seem generous enough for the serving of dip.

Dinners are competently prepared if uninspired. *Moussaka* was tasty though somewhat dry. *Shish kebab* ($12.75) was tender and flavorful, though served with a rather thick and salty sauce better left on the side. *Teriyaki* chicken ($10.95) also suffered from salty sauce, though the meat was very soft and moist. The large Mediterranean platter featured some very crisp deep fried calamari.

When we visited Makai with a group of very hungry children, a tough test for any restaurant, we found service slower than we needed. Soup and salad came slowly, and the bread basket contained only three slices. That left two empty hands! Our waitress agreed to bring another basket, but it too contained only three slices, and by this time, some of the first hands were already out for seconds. The math of the three slices just never worked for us! On the next table, we saw a basket containing three slices even though only one person was eating! It may be that, no matter how many you are, the bread counter only makes it to three!

Makai offers an interesting menu, and the people are friendly and hardworking. Pick a cool night, arrive in multiples of three, ask for sauce to be served in a side dish, and keep sending the bread basket back to the kitchen!

On Rt 56 in Kapa'a, opposite Kapa' Beach Park. 822-3955. Full bar. Credit cards. 10 % senior discount. Children's menu. Map: 5

Ma's Family, Inc.

Ma's tiny luncheonette is so far off the beaten path in Lihue that you'd probably never find it if you didn't stumble onto it by chance. For the past 18 years, Ma's family has established a reputation for well-priced and well-cooked breakfasts and lunches, and you'll probably find the dozen tables filled with local people on their way to work in the morning or stopping off for lunch.

The few tourists who happen onto it will love Ma's expertly cooked eggs, delicious pancakes and waffles that one babysitter described as "about the best." The menu, which is posted on the wall over the pass-through to the kitchen, also lists some Hawaiian dishes, for example roast *kalua* pig that shredded perfectly for our little ones to pick up with their fingers. Even the toast is excellent. Corned beef hash lovers may find Ma's version too much like a potato pancake, but the fried *min* noodles accompanied by eggs and sausage may open your eyes to new possibilities for breakfast.

Service is fast and extremely friendly in the sunny, spartan dining room. Coffee arrives immediately in a large carafe and the food shortly thereafter. If you don't like canned milk in your coffee, ask for a small glass of the fresh stuff. When you leave, you'll be astonished to find how little your meal has cost you. When three adults and four children can breakfast for less than $20, you feel like popping into the kitchen to give Ma a big hug! And many of our readers agree!

4277 Halenani St in Lihue (enter between BJ Furniture and Lihue Furniture on Rice St). Cash only. Daily 5 am-1:30 pm. Weekends 12:30 am to 10 am. Coffee or tea are free with breakfast! Map: 4

Norberto's El Cafe

After many comfortable years in an old luncheonette tucked under the wing of the Roxy Theater, Norberto's has moved to more modern quarters on the main street of Kapa'a. The dining room is attractively laid out on two levels separated by beams and railings like a patio. White stucco walls and woodgrain tables create a setting like a cantina, colorfully decorated with hanging plants, sombreros, and gas lamps. Trophies won by the girls' softball team, coached by Norberto, sit atop a piano, where guests occasionally contribute to the informal atmosphere with impromptu entertainment.

Over the years, prices have not changed much, and almost everything is very reasonable. Bud on tap, served in a full pitcher with iced beer mugs, is only $4.50. Margaritas go for $1.50 (or $2.50 in a beer mug and $8.50 for a pitcher!), and even the Taylor California Cellars at $5/carafe is bargain priced.

El Cafe offers a variety of inexpensive *a la carte* entrees as well as 6 complete Mexican dinners with soup, vegetable, beans, chips and salsa for $9.95 or less. Delicious guacamole is only $1.50, or half price with a dinner! Terrific nachos ($2.00/small) are generously covered with cheese. When we finished our bean soup ($1.75), we were asked if we wanted seconds!

The *Burrito El Cafe* ($6.95) deserves to be called a house specialty—the *tortilla* generously stuffed with flavorful beef, beans and cheese, baked *enchilada* style and topped with *guacamole* and the freshest red tomatoes and lettuce. On the full dinner menu, the *tostada* ($8.95) was a huge colorful salad mounded over a crisp *tortilla*, and the *Chili Relleno* ($8.95) is dipped (not drowned) in egg and gently cooked, so that it comes out light, tender and delicately flavored. Meat dishes can also be ordered vegetarian style. For the some who like it hot, plenty of homemade salsa is on the table to add to your dishes, and the chef will be happy to say *"Ole!"* to any challenge!

Service is extremely friendly, and children are treated with tolerance, even when cranky. On our last visit, when the salsa proved too hot for the short people to handle, the waitress immediately brought a bowl of bean soup to our table. As soon as the kids started dipping their chips, all you could hear was happy crunching!

4-1373 Kuhio Hwy, (cross street: Kukui St) in the heart of historic Kapa'a town. 822-3362. 5:30-9:30 pm daily. Children's complete dinners $4.50. Coffee $.75. Map: 5

Olympic Cafe

For years, the Olympic Cafe looked too modern for weather-beaten old Kapa'a. Clean paint and windows shaped like Japanese lanterns right next door to ramshackle roofs and rusted Coca Cola signs?

But the Olympic was just ahead of its time, and proves once more that, if you are patient, the world will catch up with you. Kapa'a has now been discovered as "quaint," and as the town enters the tourist era with a spurt of building and renovation, it's just catching up with the Olympic and a hard working Japanese family with foresight! And now, time has caught up with the Olympic—again! As its facade continues to weather with sun and salt, the Olympic may turn out to be Kapa'a's first modern-day antique!

Inside, the tan and white room is comfortably cool with fly fans, the woodgrain formica tables roomy. Prices are reasonable. For $1.95, you can have the breakfast special—2 pancakes, an egg, and 2 strips of bacon, just enough to make short people cheerful. The corned beef hash is a bit heavy on the potatoes, but still tasty. Coffee is excellent, though you have to settle for Royal Danish creamer or order a side of milk! For a quick meal on a morning when you want to play with the sand rather than your silverware, the Olympic may be your best bet!

Rt 56, in Kapa'a. Breakfast and lunch 7 am-2 pm daily. Dinner 5-9 pm. Coffee $.50. Lunch and dinner daily. Map: 5

Ono Char Burger

For years, a tiny shack next to the general store at Anahola was famous among local people for delicious hamburgers and fresh fruit smoothies. As more tourists heard about the hamburgers, the shack, and Duane's reputation, got larger. Picnic tables were added under the tree, and the menu was expanded. Even if the recent coat of paint doesn't quite catapult Duane's into the same league as McDonald's, the facade has certainly become brighter.

Even though Duane has sold the business, the burgers are still famous. These oversized creations, which can be made with various cheeses (even blue cheese) or teriyaki style, are priced from $3.65 to $4.40. Children can order hamburgers ($2.50) or deep fried chicken strips and fries ($2.95) that will make the rest of the party want to order the adult portion($6.75). Fries ($1.40) are excellent, sizzling hot and golden crisp.

Service can be slow, particularly at peak lunchtime. Be patient, and pack up your sandwiches (each half will be separately wrapped) and head for beautiful Anahola Beach just a mile down Aliomanu Road.

Rt 56 in Anahola. Open daily 10 am to 6 pm (Sunday 11 am to 6 pm). Cash only. Map: 5

Ono Family Restaurant

Ono Family Restaurant specializes in wholesome, inexpensive family fare. Breakfasts are well-cooked, attractively served, and generous, including some house specialties which are really special. Eggs Vegie ($4.75) is a version of eggs benedict with fresh sauteed zucchini instead of meat. Pancakes ($2.55/adult; $1.50/ child)) were voted "Ex!" by our kids, and the ham and cheese omelette ($5.35) was soft and delicious. Our waitress was very helpful with things like crackers, straws, extra napkins and extra cups for tastes of grown-up coffee—those etceteras of family dining that don't seem essential until they're missing.

For lunch, children's plates are a bargain and include a a cup of soup and a beverage. A children's chicken platter ($3.50), for example, includes a leg and thigh baked in a sweet barbecue sauce. Adults will find the hamburgers, priced from $3.65 ($2.50/

child), on the whole competently cooked, and anyone on a diet will be pleased with the vegie combo sandwich ($4.55) served on wheat branola bread. The buffalo burgers (from $5.25) are more lean and healthy than beef for the cholesterol-conscious, and their distinctive flavor will please some but not others (and unfortunately not our children)! You might also try the delicious Portuguese bean soup ($1.55), spicy with sausage, beans and macaroni. French fries are hot and crispy;lemonade is the real thing!

The restaurant has a cozy, friendly atmosphere. Wooden booths shine with polish, and many feature a partition which can be removed in order to connect two together and seat a large family like ours. Gold carpeting, pleasant yellow walls with paneling, cheerful curtains, and flowers make the dining room attractive. Family antiques harmonize with a homey assortment of square and round tables. Air conditioning keeps temperatures comfortable.

Although at times service can be painfully slow, everyone is friendly and cooperative. While you wait, children can work on pencil puzzles provided on their menus, and people seem ready to help with each other's restless little ones. On one occasion, when we could not find our waitress to get a glass of water that had suddenly become an urgent necessity, an adjacent Daddy passed over an extra. Just outside the open door, two old timers shared their donuts with our wandering seven-year-old, patted her head as she chewed, and listened politely to her latest fish story.

4-1292 Kuhio Hwy, Kapa'a. 7 am - 9 pm except Mondays. Closed Sundays at 2 pm. Credit cards. 822-1710. Map: 5

A Pacific Cafe

A Safeway shopping center is an unlikely spot for a gourmet restaurant, almost as unlikely in fact as finding a Safeway shopping center at all on a remote Pacific island. Wherever you would find it, however, A Pacific Cafe would be a special place, because Jean-Marie Josselin is a genuinely gifted chef and creates a truly unique cuisine, blending the culinary traditions of Europe and the Pacific Rim, while emphasizing the freshest of local ingredients.

As you enter the air-conditioned dining room, you will probably see him hard at work behind a tall counter pass-through, or at least you'll see his immaculate white *toque*. That is appropriate, for the chef rather than anything else is the centerpiece of this restaurant.

A Pacific Cafe realizes Josselin's dream to follow his own inspirations rather than simply implement the ideas of others. His menu changes daily, with the handful of main selections (lamb, beef, poultry, fish) presented in different preparations, so that each of your visits can be a new adventure. Each aspect of the dining experience receives exceptional attention. The plates, for example, are created by his wife, Sophronia. No two are alike in shape or color, and they frame the appetizers and entrees like culinary paintings.

You will be delighted with the ingenious, sometimes whimsical, artistry of each dish. For example, spring rolls arrive on a triangular plate with gaily colored edges, the four crispy halves standing at different heights like a mini citiscape, served in a small lake of sauce garnished with sesame seeds toasted black. Or imagine *sashimi* served *tempura* style, the *ahi* wrapped in seaweed, then deep fried and sliced in elegant, dainty medallions, the fish cool in the center, the wrapping crisp outside. Three steamed white dumplings of chicken and shrimp ($6.50), spicy and tender, appear on a colorful rectangular platter. Even something quite ordinary, like a green salad ($3.50) looks like kaleidoscope of greens, and the centerpiece of the tomato salad ($5.95) is a sphere of thin skinless slices resembling the whole tomato. *Ahi* salad is both elegant and truly wonderful. Lemon soup ($3.50) served in a lovely bowl has a distinctive fragrance and flavor.

 This is a place to venture into new territory. Even if eggplant is not your favorite vegetable, for example, try it, because this spectacular grilled Japanese eggplant with goat cheese and chili pepper vinaigrette ($6.25) may change your mind forever! Scallop ravioli with Chinese parsley sauce ($5.75) is incredibly flavorful, garnished with orange caviar and thin sliced scallions. Peking duck with shrimp taco is served with papaya ginger salsa ($7.95) appears on a bed of lettuce with a shredded carrot nest. Even familiar entrees appear in arresting fashion.   Rack of lamb, served in four generous, succulent chops, is crowned with a bird's nest of golden–fried angel hair potatoes. Tender, flavorful steak is arrayed in lovely slices with an excellent barbecue sauce.

But delicious as these entrees are, the real stars on the menu are the fresh fish, and they are truly magical—sizzling hot, meltingly tender, and enhanced with wonderful sauces. Try fresh *ahi* served with a mango and lime sauce so wonderful that it seems to release some hidden splendor in the fish itself. You may find steamed *onaga* served in a banana leaf with Kauai clams and a ginger and cilantro sauce ($18.75). Grilled *ehu* is sauteed to crispy perfection and paired with an asparagus vinaigrette. Seared swordfish arrives with a delicious garlic basil sauce ($18.50). Best of all is a peppered Hawaiian salmon with a cucumber salsa and tomato gazpacho sauce ($19.50). Attention to detail makes each aspect of the dinner special. Rice arrives in a bamboo steamer, and even the muffins are out of the ordinary—light ,tasty and flavored with herbs. Desserts are delicious and inventive , like *creme brulee* flavored with *lillikoi*, served creamy rather than thick, with a crispy browned top .

The elegant dining room has a southwestern flair, reflecting the chef's years in Los Angeles. Elegant black lacquer chairs surround the polished wood tables, set with black bamboo placemats, shining crystal, and what can only be described as *bonsai* cactus . Unlike most restaurants, where the art on the walls is merely decorative, Pacific Cafe's walls seem almost like a gallery, and in fact the 'exhibition ' changes at regular intervals. The only disadvantage in the air-conditioned room is the noise. This cafe is really best on an a night when it's not busy, if you can find one! When a restaurant makes it to Sunset Magazine, you should expect it to be jammed!

A Pacific Cafe's *a la carte* menu can be expensive, but you don't really mind paying for a meal so memorable. And actually, the fresh island fish entrees cost less than at a restaurant of comparable quality like the Westin's Inn on the Cliffs, or even at a seafood restaurant where the cuisine is more ordinary, like the nearby Seashell of Kapaa Fish and Chowder House.So, for a truly magical dining treat, don't miss A Pacific Cafe!

Kauai Village Shopping Center, Rt 56, Waipouli. Reservations essential: 822-0013. Credit cards. Map: 5

Panda Garden

Next to the Safeway in the Kauai Village Shopping Center, Panda Garden looks clean and attractive. Tables with white cloths covered with shiny glass tops make the white painted dining room look cheerful and bright. Bamboo, favorite taste treat of the panda, is the main the decorative motif.

To the strains of light rock music, perhaps the voice of Carly Simon, you consider the menu, with most choices priced between $6 and $9. Scallop soup ($7.25) was hot, thick and tasty and seemed to indicate a great meal ahead. Special Panda Garden Noodles ($6.95) recommended by our waiter, was somewhat salty, however.

Roast duck ($6.25) was tasty, though rather greasy and difficult to handle. We found service slow, but pleasant and polite.

At Panda Garden, the view is not special, the decor is not special, the service is not special, and the food is not special. Prices are reasonable, but if you are looking for inexpensive Chinese food and don't mind a shopping center location, you might consider Dragon Inn down the road.

In the Kauai Village Shopping Center, Kuhio Highway, Wailua.

The Planter's Restaurant

Just a few feet off Rt 56 at Hanama'ulu, The Planter's Restaurant is in an improbable spot for a restaurant featuring patio dining. The patio is probably cooler than the interior in summer, but its location next to the parking lot gives diners an excellent view of the cars. Inside this historic plantation building is a dining room ventilated by ceiling fans and decorated with sugar plantation memorabilia—machinery parts and tools, horse collars and ox yokes, and even a red wagon wheel hung with lanterns and plants. Candles shine on wood plank tables, and at the rear, two private booths with black leatherette seats cozy up to an indoor waterfall.

More than a dozen dinners range from $9.95 for chicken teriyaki up to $24.95 for steak and lobster. Entrees come with soup or salad, as well as rice, potato, or a somewhat garlicky pasta with romano cheese. Children can choose prime rib, chicken or shrimp dinners for only $7.50, and the boneless chicken breast passed the most stringent "no–yuk" test from the small picky eaters. For the first course, you get a bowl, which can be filled with either salad or a seafood chowder. Beef vegetable soup was peppery and extremely thick, with flavor and consistency of pot roast gravy. The dinner salad included carrots, cucumbers and tomatoes. You also get french bread, toasted with or without garlic, but the absence of bread plates means that in short order you'll have crumbs skittering everywhere.

We found house specialty prime rib to be tasty and tender, served with good *au jus* but no bone, and certainly reasonably priced at $14.95. The portion can be quite small, however, especially for children. And if you have your heart set on this dish, call ahead to reserve a portion, so you won't be disappointed. Steamed lobster tail, was tender though not distinctive enough to merit the $19.95 price. Scampi ($14.95) were large and tender, though a minimal portion of only 5 shrimp. An average size New York steak ($15.95) was tasty though with some gristle. The fresh *ono* was dry and tough though the price ($11.95) was reasonable and the portion generous. The wine list is basic Beringer, with the top-priced a Chardonnay at $19.

Service is as variable as the meals. On our last visit, our waitress had little patience for the children, and couldn't understand why we complained about sitting next to smokers on the so-called 'non-smoking' patio.

The Planter's Restaurant is obviously not the place to order an expensive meal. Your plan should be to spend as little possible and to stick to the basics, like the chicken and prime rib. In fact, some of our local friends recommend the prime rib sandwich, a bargain at only $8.95.

On Rt 56 in Downtown Hanama'ulu. 245-1606. Dinner nightly 5 - 9:45 pm. Children (under 12): chicken, fish, prime rib $7.50. Coffee: $1. Map: 4

Prince Bill's, Westin Kauai

At Prince Bill's, you will be dining at the only penthouse restaurant on Kauai. On the top floor of the Westin's tower, the dining room has a sweeping view of Kalapaki Bay, and from a window table, you can watch the waves roll in slender lines of foam and break far below you. The room is lovely, although you will find it hard to take your eyes off the view, especially in moonlight, when clouds rimmed with silver steal silently across the sky to hide the moon. In another moment, the moon escapes to light the glistening sea and cast lovely moonshadows on the gardens below. Prince Bill's enjoys this spectacular perch because the tower, part of the old Kauai Surf Hotel, was built before strict zoning regulations limited construction to four stories—"no higher than a coconut tree."

Prince Bill's peach and white decor emphasizes the spaciousness of the tall ceilings and of the two-level design of the dining room which allows almost everyone a gorgeous view. Even better, when the giant windows are open, you can enjoy wonderful breezes as well as sounds of the surf.

Prince Bill's is especially lovely at Sunday brunch. As you look down on palm trees and golden sand and feel the gentle morning breezes, you'll be thinking of all you want to do at the beach, although it's hard to leave a buffet with so many delicious creations. You'll find strawberry blintzes and baked apples, smoked salmon with capers, Banger and link sausages, wonderful fresh fruits and juices, fabulous pastries and fruit breads, or an omelette created before your eyes with your favorite cheeses and vegetables. Or try eggs benedict, fresh *onaga* with ginger, *sushi* or *sashimi*, or roast crispy duck. A server will carve a prime rib roast, or an entire roast pig to eat with steamed Chinese buns and *hoisin* sauce.

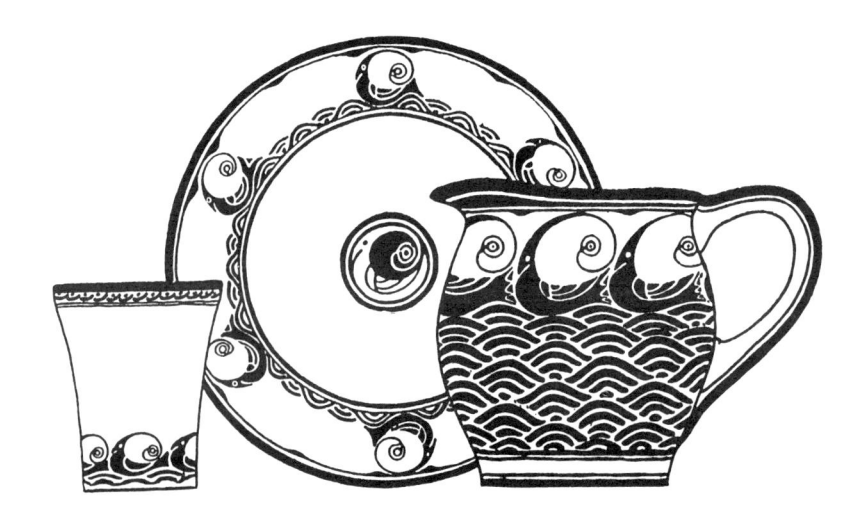

Brunch is not only delicious but elegantly served on white linen tablecloths set with fresh flowers. Champagne arrives in lovely glasses, and the staff is exceptionally friendly and helpful, especially to children who need assistance carrying plates. Our nine-year-old could not believe her eyes when the catsup she requested was ceremoniously carried to the table balanced on a tiny saucer! These little people on their best behavior were also delighted when our cordial waiter, Gerald, served hot chocolate to each one in a miniature silver pot. Afterwards, while parents enjoy the champagne and count the waves rolling into the bay, youngsters can go downstairs to explore the pool, and this excursion is an adventure in itself, as they have to follow complex directions based on the color of the columns! For all this entertainment, the price ($21.95 for adults; $12.50 for children) seems well worth it.

At dinner, Prince Bill's looks like a different restaurant. Evening breezes make the candle flames dance romantically in their glass holders, and windows open to the starry sky, with moonlight floating like a silver net across the sea.

Prince Bill's has tried several menus, the most recent featuring Italian cuisine with prices that seem more reasonable until you add in the 'antipasto bar' ($7.50). Full dinners cost between $19 (NY steak) and $23 (grilled lamb chops). Entree choices include steaks, fresh fish, chicken, lamb, and seafood. The antipasto bar is a lavish spread of fresh vegetables and salads, *ahi sashimi* and *calamari*, cold cuts, and a mountain of cooked shrimps served in the shell with cocktail sauce. Eating them is sticky business, which makes you grateful for the hot towels that follow! The antipasto bar might also make an excellent light supper ($14.50 *a la carte*).

A fresh-baked Italian loaf is served with virgin olive oil as well as an enormous baked garlic, which will please some but not all. Delicious coconut bread arrives with fragrant orange honey butter, so much like pound cake that you could save it for dessert instead of visiting the dessert bar ($4.50) where too many delicious looking pastries are full of too many calories for comfort! We tried a sensational cream tart topped with four perfectly ripe, perfectly round balls of papaya. After dinner, you can linger over delicious coffee, listen to Hawaiian melodies, and gaze out at sea.

The kitchen does very well with the new menu. Fresh pasta, supplied by *Pasta D'Oro*, is wonderful. Tomato *penne* with *porcini* mushrooms and sun dried tomatoes and *mascarpone* cheese with *pancetta* was nothing short of spectacular, the most memorable pasta we tried on the island. *Fettuccini* with seafood and the light cream sauce was delicately flavored with cheese and garlic. Entrees were also excellent. Two generous 3-bone lamb chops ($23) were perfectly crisp yet moist, very tender and tasty with a fresh rosemary sauce. Fresh *onaga* was amazing, cooked at our request in "nothing" and yet perfectly moist and flaky, with a delicious fennel butter on the side. With the entrees come ripe tomatoes *provencale*; thin, very flaky *au gratin* potatoes attractively served in a copper pan, and fresh vegetables, in our case ginger carrots and sugar peas with straw mushrooms and onions. Service is skilled as well as friendly. Your meal is never hurried, though you might ask for a break between the appetizer and entrees just to be sure.

Prince Bill's offers a unique and spectacular setting, delicious food, and polite, professional service. The menu is not inexpensive, but you get a good value for your money, and you will most likely remember an evening of good food laced with romantic images—the sounds of the sea, the foam on the waves, and the touch of tropical evening breezes.

In the Westin Kauai Hotel. Reservations necessary. 245-5050. Informal attire. Credit cards. Map: 4

The Seashell

For many years, the Seashell was the only seafood specialty restaurant on the eastern shore. With competition growing, however, the Seashell has undergone a renovation, including an update on its menu, which is now larger and includes entrees for the ten-and-under set. A new wine list offers 25 wines, most from California and most priced around $20. You could hardly call this menu inexpensive, however. Fresh fish is still $17.50 and the least expensive entree is a seafood pasta dish for $12.95.

We started with *sashimi*, a generous portion of thinly sliced *ahi* which was meltingly tender. Deep fried *calamari* ($3.95) served in a large white shell was crisp and tasty. Deep fried zucchini ($3.75) was hot and moist, although retaining a bit too much oil for first-rate "tempura-style" as described in the menu. As a better complement to its delicate flavor, you might request the sauce for *sashimi* instead of the strong cocktail sauce which comes with it.

A better choice on the complete dinner than the rather bland seafood chowder, the salad bar is extensive, and everything is attractively displayed—huge bowls of fresh spinach and lettuce, large clam shells filled very red tomatoes, fresh vegetables, giant mushrooms *vinaigrette*, pasta and vegetable salads.

The kitchen specializes in fresh fish, and we have learned over the years to avoid any dishes which require sauces or subtlety, for seasoning is often heavy handed. This was true with the *ono*, which was perfectly cooked, but much better without the strong wine and butter sauce that came with it. *Ahi* was also excellent, with no bitter taste of the grill, flaky, moist and tender. We enjoyed the scallops sauteed with mushrooms, vegetables and ginger ($19.25), for the scallops were tasty and not overcooked, and the sauce enhanced rather than disguised their flavor. *Cioppino* ($18.25) was another excellent choice, the fish, clams, shrimps and scallops cooked only to tenderness, and the broth piquant and light, colorful with snow peas, celery, carrots and onions. The New York steak arrived perfectly cooked, tender and juicy, though a bit small (8 oz for $17.75).

Despite its modest, unpretentious exterior, The Seashell is not inexpensive when you add in appetizers, cocktails, coffee and dessert. If your mood is informal, it may be just the right place, for the food is fine, the dining room pleasantly decorated, and the service friendly. If you're looking for something special, however, and are willing to drive a mile north, consider A Pacific Cafe in the Kauai Village Center.

On Rt 56 in Wailua, opposite Coco Palms Hotel. Reservations essential (request a window table but be prepared to wait for it): 822-4921. Credit cards. Dinner 5:30–10 pm daily. Children's menu: chicken nuggets, "spaghettietti", hamburger with fries for $6 or less. Low sodium, low cholesterol preparations upon request. Map: 5

Sharky's Fishmarket

You won't wonder very long about the name of this restaurant, for the first thing you'll probably see as you walk in is a shark, swimming straight towards you and leading with its mouth, directly up to the glass wall of a giant tank. Truly a memorable sight!

Don't let the shark distract your attention from the view beyond the tank, one of the most striking and panoramic ocean views of any restaurant on Kauai! It's best in daylight, so consider coming for lunch and dining outdoors on the lanai. Just keep in mind that, since the restaurant is right beneath the approach to the airport, you'll be able to count the jets (sometimes at least 4 per meal!) as they swoop in just over your head.

At dinner, the fish tank offers the brightest light in the room, and the captive sharks seem to float eerily in the dark. In fact, you'll find sharks almost everywhere—stuffed and mounted on walls or captured in mid-glide and suspended from the ceiling of Sharky's two–tiered dining room. Comfortable booths line the walls of the upper level, and on the lower one, polished wood tables with captain's chairs gleam pleasantly in candlelight. When full, however, the dining room can be quite noisy.

Compared to other restaurants at the Westin, the menu seems reasonably priced and offers a wide range of local fresh fish ($19.95) and "fresh frozen" seafood, as well as jet–set steamed clams and raw oysters, smoked fish and baked shellfish. Those who would rather die than eat something that once had fins can order an "All American Cheeseburger" ($6.95) or chicken ($10.95). Appetizers range around $10. Clam chowder ($1.95/cup) is tasty, even a bit spicy, though overly thick. *Sashimi* is excellent, meltingly soft and fragrant, a generous portion for the price.

One wonders why the Westin would open a second seafood restaurant so close to the very successful Inn on the Cliffs. The answer is that Sharky's is not operated by the Westin, but by the TJ Company which owns Duke's and Keoki's. Like them, Sharky's is informal, noisy, and gives the impression of high volume. While Inn on the Cliffs is elegant in decor and service, at Sharky's you sacrifice some of the amenities in service and presentation. Waitpersons seem rushed and unwilling to help tailor menu choices to your specific preferences. Cole slaw is served in a puddle right next to your entree on your plate. Salad is romaine lettuce with the house dressing as the only choice.

Preparation of entrees, particularly those requiring delicate seasoning, is uneven. Fresh *mahi mahi*, usually so delicate and flaky, was tough and tasteless when we tried it. Fresh *onaga* and *opakapaka*, on the other hand, were perfectly sauteed, though one was served in a sauce with too many strongly flavored chunks of ginger. *Ahi teriyaki* was well prepared, the portion generous. Seafood *marinara* was tasty, but slender on the fish, and the shrimps could have been more tender. *Cioppino* was so heavy on the tomatoes that you could not taste the seafood, which was also somewhat tough.

Unless everyone eats cheeseburgers or chicken, families can soon run up an expensive tab with *a la carte* extras. There's no question, though, that kids would love the layout—the shave ice booth by the door and the sharks swimming in the tank. And everyone will enjoy riding the Westin's Venetian launch across the lagoon before and after dinner (Check the time of the last boat departure). Adults interested in a romantic evening, however, might prefer to spend a few dollars more at the Inn on the Cliffs, and enjoy more attentive service, more quiet dining, more elegant surroundings, and consistently prepared fresh fish.

In the Westin Kauai. Reservations necessary: 246-4770. Ride the launch (free) across the lagoon or take the hotel mini bus, or drive directly to Fashion Landing. Dinner nightly. Credit cards. Children: hamburger $4.95, *teriyaki* chicken sandwich $8.95. Map: 4

The Sizzler

From the road, the Sizzler's pink neon sign makes a strong statement. Beneath that sign, however, we found a sizzling disappointment! First, you must stand on line, wait while an employee takes down the orders of everyone ahead of you, and pay – in cash – while your order is called into the kitchen at the register. With receipt in hand, you find a table, then visit the famous salad bar which costs extra unless you are a senior citizen. That much is predictable. The rest is up to chance. Your food may be brought out too soon or, if the restaurant is full, later than you'd like, and as we found on two occasions, without everything you ordered, so don't lose that proof of purchase in the salad dressing!

And prices are deceptive. What looks like a great buy on the sign outside (Prime Rib Dinner $9.99) is, according to our waiter, only 8 oz—not much to look at on the plate, and it's $3.99 more if you add the salad bar. If you add the salad bar charge to the larger prime rib ($17.99), you'll actually pay a whopping $19.99 — more than you would at the Bull Shed ($17.95) — which offers a free salad bar and also table service — and also more than the 26 ounce portion of prime ribs served at Duke's at the Westin Kauai.

The salad bar ($7.49 *a la carte*) is the best deal in the house. At $3.99, children under 12 have it even better, as that modest price includes even a small beverage. The salad bar offers hot soup, fruits, a completely furnished *taco* bar with *taco* and *tostada* shells, as well as hot pasta.

At breakfast, you'll find the same line, the same system, and the same problems. Food orders don't always arrive at the same time, and service is uneven. When our older children went to Sizzler on a great adventure—breakfast without Mom and Dad—even they had mixed experiences. One morning, the waiter offered them fruit from the salad bar when their breakfasts were delayed more than twenty minutes. Another morning, however, the waitress brought the wrong order for one child, and cold eggs for the others. She whisked the eggs back to the kitchen, but the eggs came back reheated rather than re-cooked. At that point, the children told her, with all the grave politeness of short people trying to act tall, that the eggs were as hard as rocks and the papaya slices were hot. When the waitress informed them that eggs could not be returned more than once, she entered our family folklore forever!

At the Sizzler, you have to work for what you eat, and dining is rushed rather than relaxed. As in many fast food outlets, you'll find the dining room clean and bright, but it's hard to imagine wanting to linger over coffee for very long. You end up, in our opinion, paying too much for too little, and all of it in precious vacation cash. For these reasons, we found the Sizzler, alas, to be a fizzler!

On Rt 56 in Wailua. No reservations or credit cards. Wine, cocktails, and beer. Breakfast, lunch, and dinner daily. Map: 5

Sumo Restaurant

In the Kukui Grove Shopping Center, Sumo offers reasonably priced lunches in a pleasant and attractive setting. The lavender and white decor, accented by leafy green plants, looks clean and crisp; *shoji* screens soften the lighting and mute the traffic noises in the mall.

The menu offers a wide variety of sandwiches, salads, and Oriental dishes. Prices are reasonable, and so is the quality of what you are served. Oriental dishes are hot and colorful with vegetables, though the taste is on the bland side. Combination lunch plates include an excellent *miso* soup, a better choice than the rather small saucer of Romaine that passes for the house salad. You can choose from a wide array of *sushi*.

Some dishes are surprises, like crispy, tasty chicken wings. Others are more ordinary, including fairly pedestrian sandwiches. Shrimp *tempura* may seem more like deep fried shrimp in bread crumbs, though it is accompanied by stir–fried noodles with carrots, squash, and green beans with two scoops of rice for only $7. Portions are large, and children can choose chicken, cheeseburger, or hot dog with rice or fries and a drink for less than $4.

While the food may suffer from one–dimensional seasoning, Sumo Restaurant offers a good value for your money in a setting more pleasant than you'd expect in a shopping center. When you're tired of hitting the stores, it's a good place to rest your feet without wrestling with your wallet.

In the Kukui Grove Center, Lihue. Open for breakfast, lunch, dinner daily. 246-0113. Credit cards. Air conditioned. Map: 4

Tempura Garden,
Westin Kauai Hotel

At Tempura Garden, the Westin has bypassed the tradition of Benihana in favor of the tradition of *kaiseki,* the exquisitely fine dining developed over centuries by Kyoto's noble class. Ceremony and presentation are as important as what is eaten, and each element of the meal is carefully chosen as part of the total composition of color, texture and taste. Ingredients are the finest and freshest of the season; natural flavors and colors are enhanced rather than disguised by seasonings; and every aspect of the meal is designed to achieve an elegant simplicity which belies the extraordinary effort involved in the preparation.

The Kyoto *kaiseki* dinner ($59), is a sequence of thirteen courses including appetizer, sliced raw fish, clear soup, *tempura*, broiled selection, vinegared salad, steamed rice, pickled vegetables, a final soup, fresh fruit desert, ceremonial green tea, and confectionery. From start to finish of this extraordinary dining experience, the colors and shapes delight the eye while tastes and textures intrigue the palate. Our first course, a fish cake topped with sea urchin roe, was delicate and light. Next came sliced raw fish, both *ahi* (yellow fin tuna) and a deliciously subtle white fish (yellow tail), the translucent slices arranged on single leaf of *shiso,* an herb with a wonderful fragrance of mint and anise. Our third course was a clear soup with a single, floating fish cake. Our broiled entree, pink snapper, was perfectly cooked, very sweet, and garnished with pungent shredded *shiitake* mushrooms. *Tempura* followed, impossibly light, almost confections of shrimp and white fish, eggplant and mushrooms. The vinegar salad of clam, shrimp and persimmon was a piquant counterpoint, and then the 'final soup,' richly flavored miso soup served warm rather than hot, and white rice in a lacquer bowl.

The *kaiseki* dinner is clearly not for everyone! To make dining more accessible, the menu has been expanded to include four additional, and less costly, dinners, as well as many *a la carte* choices. The *Tempura* Dinner is a seven-course meal priced according to different entree selections ($24-$38). In the *Yakimono* dinner, the entree course is a broiled fresh fish, chicken, or teriyaki beef ($28-$31). *Nabemono* dinners offer entrees cooked at the table. Choices include *Sukiyaki,* with beef ($33) or chicken ($28) cooked with vegetables in a flat iron pan and seasoned with sweetened soy sauce; *Shabu Shabu,* ($33), thinly sliced beef cooked with vegetables in a traditional Japanese pot and served with a *shoyu* and citrus sauce or a *miso* sesame sauce; or *Okisuki,* ($37), a seafood assortment.

No matter which entree you choose, you will find wonderful accompaniments: shredded chicken artfully arranged with Japanese radish and red caviar; or possibly some tender poached chicken, skewered shrimp and a single quail egg.

You can also can also order a wonderful meal by combining *a la carte* choices. Delicious fresh broiled *onaga* costs less by itself ($22), and to round off your dinner you can add a spectacular *miso* soup ($4.50) and white rice ($2). You can also choose from a wonderful array of *tempura* selections at $2.50 each, or from *sushi* created by a master Japanese chef.

The dining room has the understated elegance suitable as a backdrop for the spectacular colors and artistic presentation of the cuisine. Plain wood floors and black granite counters and tabletops seem at once luxurious and spare. Everything is also authentic, from the elegant Japanese china to the lacquer platters painted with a single white orchid to mark each diner's place. Half of the dining takes place at a long counter, where people who sit side by side can watch the chefs slice and chop and make things sizzle.

At Tempura Garden, the cuisine is highly specialized as well as expensive. Surprisingly, it's the only indoor Westin restaurant that is not air-conditioned. Fly fans can usually keep the air moving, although, when the windows are open, the sound of water splashing in the garden outside can be distracting. If you enjoy Japanese cuisine, Tempura Garden offers superb cuisine and elegant service—a meal you'd find nowhere else on Kauai.

Reservations 245-5050. Free valet parking. Dinner nightly except Tuesdays, 5:00 pm to 9:30 pm. Credit cards. Map: 4

Tip Top Motel

With a name like Tip Top, this combination motel, restaurant, and bakery conjures up certain expectations: a clean room for under $20, a square meal for under $5. But you're not really sure that you should believe in this any more than you would in the tooth fairy! It is true, though. Since 1916, the Tip Top Motel has served fairly-priced, honest and unpretentious food, and for this reason, is more popular with local people than the tourists who manage to find it on the side street of Lihue. The dining room is large and dimly lit, with the dull, hollow sound of a school cafeteria, but nonetheless it is comfortably air-conditioned, with booths along the wall and well spaced formica tables. The real attraction is the prices. Delicious pancakes with macadamia nuts, bananas, pineapples or raisins are only $2.25. Bacon and eggs, accompanied by a scoop of hash browns, cost $2.95. A ham and cheese omelette is $3.35. While in general the food is well-prepared if unexciting, the homemade pineapple and guava jam is special. Have it on toast, but that's *a la carte.*

Children will have fun here. They can roam around, check out the bakery display or select postcards from the rack while breakfast is being prepared. Our waitress, a grandmother who had raised twelve children of her own, was unusually tolerant, patient and kind, making an extra trip to the bakery to switch donuts when one child changed her mind and was on the verge of tears. The donuts are delicious—take some along for a snack—and be sure to sample the house specialty, macadamia nut cookies. At Tip Top, you won't find the kind of breakfasts you get at Kountry Kitchen or Eggbert's, but you won't pay their prices either. And what you do get is good enough to keep everyone cheerful—until lunch!

3173 Akahi St., Lihue. Cash only. Coffee $.60. Opens daily at 6:45 am. Map: 4

The Voyage Room,
Sheraton Coconut Beach Hotel

We're never quite sure what the menu will be at the Voyage Room, for it seems to change almost from year to year. The newest menu is the best in the last four, in our opinion. However, the restaurant's best feature—the enormous salad bar— has apparently fallen victim to high overhead.

'Sunset specials' available between 6 and 7 pm are bargain priced at $9.95. Intended to be plain cooking for those on a budget, you'll find choices like pot roast, meat loaf or pasta. The dinner menu offers the standard *a la carte* entrees priced from $10.75, as well as homemade pastas and 'sailing lightly' choices. The wine list, though unbelievably limited, is not very expensive.

Food quality remains fairly ordinary. Homemade angel hair pasta was more like vermicelli, and was both overcooked and overpriced. Thai spring rolls were thick, primarily with rice, and served with an excellent dipping sauce. The *onaga* was tasty though on the small side, and the fresh *mahi mahi* was cleanly broiled, both tender and moist, and tasty without the strongly flavored sauce which we had requested to be served on the side.

The ups and downs of this changeable restaurant have certainly kept us busy. We always look forward to our return visits, not only because we never know just what we'll find, but also because the Voyage Room is such a pleasant place for dinner and conversation. Even when full, the dining room feels uncrowded, the tall and roomy rattan chairs screening other diners from view, and the tiered arrangement of tables creating privacy. Gentle breezes from the hotel's central courtyard keep the temperature cool, and candle flames glow romantically on tables set with white linen and shining glassware. This is a place to visit when the moon is full, for you can sit on the veranda and watch the leaves dance in a luminous sky to the music of a fountain. After dinner, stroll along the beach and count the silver linings of the clouds, or watch as silver spreads across the waves when the moon steals free to light the sky.

In the Sheraton Coconut Beach, Kapa'a. Reservations 822-4422. Credit Cards. Coffee $1.25. Children's dinners on selected entrees. Map: 5

Wailua Marina Restaurant

One of the oldest restaurants on Kauai, the Wailua Marina is also one of the best inexpensive places to take the family. Though owned by relatives of the family which operates the Green Garden Restaurant in Hanapepe (You'll recognize the placemats!), the Marina has a completely separate identity and, in our opinion, much better food. The dining room is large and features an enormous mural of an underwater vista complete with stuffed fish and a turtle shell. Weather permitting, ask to sit on the large covered porch decorated with plants and fresh flowers. Cooled by delightful breezes, it looks out over the Wailua River, where boats rock gently in the docks. In the evening, candles light the tables with a golden glow, and the air is soft and fragrant.

A pleasant waitress will probably recommend the fresh fish specials, and be sure to take the advice, for the fish is usually delicious, both moist and tender. *Mahi mahi* is broiled to perfection, and the fresh *ahi* stuffed with crab ($11.25) is well seasoned and flavorful. The fresh *ono* with marina sauce ($12.75) is juicy, tender, and flaky, a generous portion of 2 large slices. A local favorite, the hot lobster salad ($4.95) is a true house specialty, a small casserole of lobster chopped with celery and mayonnaise and baked till both creamy and crispy—a much more satisfying appetizer than the rather thin clam chowder ($1.50) or the onion soup ($1) an overly salty version not unlike Lipton's. Another wonderful entree is the local slipper lobster, a sweet and tender 6 oz tail served with a filet of fresh ono ($17) and accompanied with small cups of both teriyaki sauce and drawn butter.

The menu features no fewer than 41 entrees, with most under $10. Steaks start at $10.95, and dinner includes rolls, rice or potato, a salad which can charitably be described as small, and a vegetable, in our case a third of an ear of corn resting on a bed of shredded lettuce with an orchid atop an envelope of catsup! The hot, crispy french fries are considerably better than the somewhat greasy fried rice, although even that's not too bad if you flavor it with some of the kitchen's delicious *teriyaki* sauce.

When we took the children, we were able to sample more of the menu. The kids preferred the fried chicken ($4.30) to the relatively dry *teriyaki* chicken, but they loved the *teriyaki* sauce on the side for dipping! The roast beef ($12.95) was a bit mealy though of good size. The kitchen does best with fresh fish! To keep prices this reasonable, the Marina cuts a few corners, but they're the kind no one really misses if you catch the spirit of the place. The pleasantness of the setting more than compensates for paper napkins and placemats. The salad dressing may not be quite enough for the salad which is not quite enough for the plate, but on the other hand, the rolls with whipped butter are light and fluffy and smell of the oven! If the salad dressing appears in a paper pill cup and the parmesan cheese in the kind of small envelope Lipton's uses for tea bags, just smile, for you can feed the whole family for less than you will believe possible. Prices are reasonable, portions generous, and children can chose from ten dinners for about $3 less than adult prices, which are reasonable to begin with. The 11 wines on the list are not very exciting, but there is a chardonnay by "Ernest and Julio" for only $10. Don't pass up the homemade coconut or macadamia nut pies ($1.50).

Dinner at the Wailua Marina will not cost you very much, but you'll come away well-fed and well-satisfied, with a pleasant memory of dining by candlelight, with the fragrance of flowers in the evening breeze and the lights on the river winking as the dusk deepens into night.

For breakfast, you can sit out by the boats and enjoy tasty eggs benedict ($4.50), delicious corned beef hash ($4) or bacon and eggs ($3.75). It's hot, fast, and filling—perfect for those mornings when you're on the way to the airport and need every ounce of strength to get those bags through the agriculture inspection without misplacing anything—or anybody!

Rt 56 in Wailua. 8:30 am–9 pm daily. 822-4311 (reservations and free shuttle from Wailua area hotels and condos). Map: 5

Waipouli Deli & Restaurant

Does this sound familiar? Your body clock is off. You're fully awake—and starving—3 hours early. You'll never make it till lunch, but you want to spend the morning on the beach and not in some dark, air-conditioned restaurant with poky service!

Well, the Waipouli Deli is for you! Generous portions of tasty food coupled with speedy delivery and unbeatable prices have made the Waipouli Deli a favorite spot on the east coast for local families and increasing numbers of tourists. In fact, although in the past you had to wait for a table no matter when you arrived (there were, after all, only 6 tables), the hard working Japanese owner has moved her shop to larger, more comfortable quarters to accommodate the growing clientele.

Larger it is, but it still looks like formica city, so don't go expecting orchids on the table! But though short on atmosphere, it's got a "breakfast special" deserving of the name. For $1.99, you get an egg cooked the way you like, two slices of bacon, and two pancakes—perfect for hungry children, not to mention adults. Eggs are expertly cooked, side meats not overly fatty, and pancakes light. On the lunch and dinner menus, there are lots of bargains in American and Oriental food served luncheonette style.

Service is fast, efficient, and very friendly. Children receive smiles, crackers, and once even a pencil and paper for doodling. We were in and out and on our way in less than an hour! If you want to save money and be well fed before the morning slips away from you, this is your place!

On Rt 56 in the Waipouli Town Plaza, behind McDonald's. Open 7:30 am-9:30 pm daily. 822-9311 for take-out orders. Map: 5

Fast Foods

It still seems odd to see a **McDonald's** golden arch on this remote island paradise, but in both Lihue and Kapa'a you can close you eyes as you bite down on a Big Mac and feel like you've never left home! **Burger King** and **Taco Bell** at the Kukui Grove Center will keep you from feeling too far away from it all. **Pizza Hut** delivers, and you can charge your pizza to your credit card by phone!

Some local restaurants are swift and tasty alternatives to the national chains. On the eastern shore, **Ono Family Restaurant** and the **Waipouli Delicatessan** in Kapa'a offer a bargain priced children's hamburger platter, or try the 'old fashioned ' hamburgers at **Bubba's**. At **Makai**, you can take out *gyros* or other Mediterranean specialties. **Kauai Smokehouse** near the new Wailua Safeway has delicious spicy chicken and ribs. Those who like healthful foods should stop in at **Papaya's** for wonderful salads, fresh fruits, vegetables, and muffins. Best food in the Coconut Plantation Marketplace, in Mikey's judgment, is **Aloha Kauai Pizza**, pizza with crispy crust and tasty sauce.

Our favorite family take-out spot on the eastern shore is **Ono Char Burger** (formerly Duane's) in Anahola. While service can be pokey, the terrific burgers, french fries, onion rings, and fried chicken will seem worth the wait, and you can take your order to nearby Anahola Bay and eat on the beach.

In Kilauea on the north shore, **Jacques's Bakery** on Oka Street opens at 6:30 am. Don't miss the coconut pastries (They'll be gone by noon)! Just down the street near the Kong Lung Store, **The Kilauea Bakery** features fragrant breads, rolls, cookies and even fresh pizza. You'll find deli sandwiches at **Farmer's Market**. Even better, enjoy a wonderful fresh fruit smoothie at nearby **Banana Joe's**.

In Hanalei, try **Hanalei Gourmet's** terrific sandwiches on homemade breads and rolls, or have them pack a picnic lunch for you to pick up on your way to the beach. For dessert, go next door for **Wishing Well** shave ice. Across the street at **Pizza Hanalei**, the homemade crust is crispy and the cheese and toppings generous. Next door at **Hanalei Health & Natural Foods** you'll find delicious vegetarian sandwiches. Or step up to **Tropical Taco's** famous green truck, usually parked right next to the Dolphin Restaurant near the Hanalei River.

The inexpensive (around $4) "plate lunch" is a Kauai tradition. Try one at the lunch counters at the **Big Save** Markets, or the

Dairy Queen in Lihue, where you can get *miso* soup and a salad with an entree like boiled *akule* fish that, according to one reader, "has to be tasted to be appreciated." **Kauai Chop Suey** offers a "special plate" ($4) which is almost enough to feed two, as does **Barbecue Inn**. At **Ho's Garden** in Kukui Grove Shopping Center, $4 buys a large mound of crisp cooked vegetable chop suey, rice and Chinese meat balls, or for the best in *saimin*, try **Hamura Saimin** just two blocks away. In Kapa'a, the lunch plates at **Dragon Inn** are great, or try **Restaurant Shiroma**.

On the south shore, **Brennecke's Snack Shop** can whip up delicious hamburgers and sandwiches. Just cross the street and picnic at Poipu Beach Park! In the Kiahuna Shopping Center, try **Paradise Hot Dogs** for hot dogs steamed in beer, and **Pizza Bella**. The crust is crispy, and the cheese and sauce pleased the picky eaters who don't like it too spicy. **Shipwreck Subs** lets you design a terrific sandwich with an extensive array of meats, cheese, and vegetables on delicious homemade wheat rolls. The line for these customized subs gets long at peak mealtimes. At **Garden Isle Bake Shop**, you'll find wonderful fresh baked doughnuts, pastries, and cinnamon rolls. Stop by for coffee and croissant for breakfast!

At the nearby Kukui'ula shopping center, don't miss **Taqueria Nortenos** for great Mexican take-out. **Mustard's Last Stand**, just to the west of Poipu, at the junction of Rt 50 and Rt 530, seems to have been designed with kids in mind. Hot dogs ($2.95 or $2.25 under 12), are the house specialty, along with sausages, and quarter-pound hamburgers ($3.25), with no fewer than 20 condiments, including 5 mustards, 3 cheeses, 3 kinds of onions, guacamole, salsa, and sauerkraut. While the kids are busy chewing, adults can visit a gift shop with a wide selection of shell necklaces and souvenirs at low prices. At "Geckoland Mini Golfpark" next door, kids can putt through 9 holes representing such Kauaian landmarks as "Waimea Canyon," "Sleeping Giant" and the "Tree Tunnel." It's the best dollar you'll ever spend! (9 am -7 pm daily).

South Shore Restaurants
The Beach House Restaurant

A longtime favorite of both residents and visitors, the Beach House once perched on a sea wall only inches from the waves, a great spot to watch the sun set into the ocean and enjoy perfectly cooked seafood in a relaxed and casual setting. In fact, the tables were so close to the waves, that when Hurricane 'Iwa struck Kauai in 1982, the entire restaurant was swept out to sea—leaving only the concrete slab to mark the spot where so many evenings had passed so pleasantly.

One of the original owners has rebuilt the restaurant on the old site, at a more respectful distance from the waves. Sliding glass doors open to the evening air and to spectacular views of surfers catching the waves as the sun sets into the shimmering sea. As you stroll along the walkway next to the ocean, you will find it hard to believe that tables were once as close to the rocks as your feet!

Although the new building preserves the original restaurant's casual ambiance (waitpersons wear shorts), the dining room is far more elegant. White lattice and leafy plants give the impression of a gazebo by the sea. Pink tables with green cloths and comfortable upholstered chairs are arranged in a tiered L-shaped room, where fly fans hum pleasantly to encourage evening breezes.

The menu features steak and seafood dinners, which include salad and potato or rice, and you can combine almost any two entrees into a dinner portion. Prices have gone up again, with prime rib now among the least expensive entrees at $18.50, and the most expensive, lobster tail, a whopping $27.50. Entrees are served with steamed rice, rice pilaf, french fries or baked potato, and vegetables. Dinners also include a green salad, topped with a layer of grated romana cheese and a rather vinegary house dressing, accompanied by some overly sweet fruit muffins.

As we have watched prices go up over the past few years, food quality, in our opinion, has gone steadily downward. The best we can say about what comes out of the kitchen is that it is uneven, and in fact even our waiter complained of low staff morale and ineffective management. Although we can remember dinners when the *ahi* and *ono* has been moist and flaky, on our most recent visits the fish has been disappointingly dry. Last time around the fresh *ono* ($20.50) was downright terrible, not only dry but tough and tasteless as well. Though slightly better in texture, the *mahi mahi* ($20.50) had almost no flavor.

Fresh fish tastes best when it is fresh, and it makes sense that when a restaurant is full, and the kitchen prepares a lot of fish, what arrives at your table will be of good quality. If the dining room is empty, however, you may want to think twice about fins and scales! We didn't have much better luck with meat, however. Rack of lamb ($22.50), served in separately grilled chops, was tender though bitter-tasting from the grill.

The Beach House wine list has gone from ordinary to mediocre. You'll have to spend in the $20 range for a pretty limited selection, like a Beaulieu Chardonnay for $24. Since our bottle arrived barely cool, consider ordering as soon as you arrive and start the bottle chilling in an ice bucket!

Children will like the Beach House. They get crayons and paper for doodling while waiting for their steak, fish, or chicken ($6.50). After dinner, they can run around on the lawn outside or toss stones into the water while their parents linger over coffee.

At the Beach House, the view may turn out to be the best part of your dinner, so when making your reservation, be sure to ask for a window table and insist on it when you arrive. The Beach House has one of the most beautiful settings you can imagine, one of the few that is lovely even after dark, when the last light of sunset fades and the waves begin to glisten with moonlight. We hope that management takes steps to make the meals measure up!

On Spouting Horn Road in Poipu. Reservations recommended. Request a window table, but be prepared to wait for it. 742-7575. Credit cards. Cocktails from 4 pm. Dinner 5:30-10:30 pm. Map: 3

Brennecke's Beach Broiler

Brennecke's serves the best reasonably-priced fresh seafood on the island, and there are usually four varieties to choose from. It's worth calling ahead to find out what's going to be on the menu and reserving a portion of *ulu'a* or *onaga* if available so that you won't be disappointed to find it sold out when you arrive.

In this second story restaurant across the street from Poipu Beach Park, you'll find prices modest and the atmosphere decidedly informal, so you'll feel comfortable no matter what you're wearing. But the informal ambiance is the result of the meticulous attention to detail which enhances every aspect of the dining experience. The decor, for example, looks very plain—a porch in soft grey and white tones—but everything is spanking clean, the paint still shiny and fresh looking, the chairs and grey formica tables immaculate, the flowers in the window boxes bright and cheerful. It's the kind of porch where your child could retrieve a piece of pasta from the floor and put it in his mouth and you wouldn't have to look the other way.

The food receives equal attention to detail. Clam chowder is creamy rather than thick, generous with clams, and delicately seasoned. *Teriyaki* steak stix ($7.25) are medium rare, tasty, and sizzling hot. Dinner entrees include beef, pasta, and poultry ($14.94-$21.95), as well as a host of less expensive sandwich baskets and munchies, but the fresh island fish is the reason to come to Brennecke's. Your fish will be perfectly cooked, crisp on the outside, meltingly moist and delicious inside. The secret to Brennecke's flawless broiling is the grill, designed by owner Bob

French and fueled by charcoal made from *kiawe* wood from Ni'ihau. It burns extremely hot and clean, sealing in juices quickly and leaving no aftertaste.

During our visits to Brennecke's over the years, we have been delighted with almost every fresh fish we have sampled. Even the old stand–bys, *ahi* and *ono* are so perfectly cooked that they seem extraordinary. Most recently, we tried *opakapaka*, a superb filet which could not have been juicier or tastier. Grouper, or white sea bass, with a texture somewhat like lobster, was also sensational, flaking easily and gently seasoned. If you are lucky, you will be able to sample the fresh *mahi mahi*, flaky and soft, unforgettably sweet and garnished with homemade tartar sauce. Sixteen entrees include steak, chicken, and ribs, as well as combinations. Your dinner will arrive with pasta and sauteed fresh vegetables, the carrots, zucchini, and broccoli still vivid in color. Since dinners include bread and soup or salad ($19.95), Brennecke's gives you a fair deal for great fish!

If you're not hungry enough for a full dinner, Brennecke's offers no fewer than 14 reasonably priced options, including several sandwich baskets, a huge platter of nachos ($6.25), and burgers ($6.95). Ligea's BBQ beef ribs ($14.95) can also be ordered in an appetizer-sized portion of two ribs, each meaty and meltingly tasty.

The wine list is limited, with almost all selections both inexpensive and ordinary, the best a Murphy Goode chardonnay at $23.95. Children can choose from seven dinners, like mini-pizza ($4.95) or teriyaki steak ($7.25) of fresh fish ($10.95), and even have chocolate milk ($1.25) or a grown-up looking fruit punch ($1.50). Kid's burgers, chicken, and fish are very successful, judging from the enthusiasm of six youngsters seated next to our table.

For the best in fresh fish, beautifully broiled and attractively served, it's hard to find a better spot than Brennecke's. The staff is friendly and professional, the dining comfortable and open to evening breezes. It may be noisy when full, but it's busy for all the right reasons. Prices are reasonable, and best of all, you can be assured that your money will buy top quality. Brennecke's is one of the most popular restaurants on the south shore, so be sure to phone ahead for a reservation if you don't want to stand in line.

Ho'one Rd. Poipu. For the daily fish report, or for reservations (necessary) 742-7588. Credit cards. A sign of the times: nine non-alcoholic "mocktails." Coffee or brewed decaf $1. Dinner 5-10:30 pm daily. Cocktails and pupus from 3 pm. Map: 3

Brick Oven Pizza

Ask just about any Kauai resident where to find the best pizza, and you'll probably hear, 'Brick Oven Pizza. ' We agree! This family owned operation in Kalaheo has been one of our most popular stops, ever since we figured out how to survive lunchtime with four hungry, and thus very cranky, children. As we leave the beach, we simply call from a pay phone, order the pizza, and find it (miraculously!) ready for us when our noisy crew arrives. We have only to cut-and-serve, and temperaments improve as quickly as those mouths can chew-and-swallow.

Brick Oven has become so successful that expansion was inevitable, and the operation moved across the road to roomier quarters. The new dining room has much of the charm of the old one, from the cheerful red–checked tablecloths to the murals of pizza serendipity—a pizza shaped like the island of Kauai, for example, with a "Garlic Grotto," a "Mushroom Valley," a "Grand Pizza Canyon," and a "Port Anchovy." Friendliness is in the air.

But good as all this is, the pizza is even better, as fine as you'll find anywhere. The homemade dough—either white or whole wheat—is simply delicious, crunchy without being dry and with a fluted crust like a pie, shiny with garlic butter. The sauce, in the words of the short judges, has "awesome spice, cooked just right"; there is lots of cheese; the Italian sausage is made right in the kitchen, and tomatoes are red, juicy and fresh. Though pizza is expensive here as everywhere on Kauai, the portions are generous and quality unbeatable. A family size (15") starts at $14.20, but you may be tempted to try one of the outrageous special creations described on the menu, the "super" ($18.50), or one of the delicious looking sandwiches made on fresh baked rolls, bargain priced at $4–$5, or a salad. You can wash it all down with ice cold beer ($3.35 for 1/2 pitcher) or soda ($3.15/ pitcher). Kids will love to watch the dough spin into pizza during that hard, hungry time of waiting,especially at peakhours when it's jammed.

At Brick Oven, you'll find a smile and pleasant word for short persons no matter how cranky. When Lauren spilled her coke, our waitress not only wiped herdry but brought her a new glass filled to the very brim! Each child can ask for a ball of pizza dough, which feels so good in the hands that it usually manages to say out of the hair—all the way home.

Rt 50 in Kalaheo. 11 am-11 pm daily. Closed Mondays. 332-8561. Closed Mondays. Coffee: $.55. Map 2

Camp House Grill

Who would think to look for one of Kauai's best hamburgers in the tiny town of Kalaheo (already sufficiently blessed, one would think, with the island's best pizza)? It's worth the drive to try a Camp House hamburger, 1/3 pound of ground chuck, served in a basket with a pile of some of the hottest, crispiest french fries you have ever tasted, and amazingly priced at $3.95.

If you were able to find Kalaheo, a tiny blip on the line of Rt 50 going west from Poipu, you would probably decide Camp House Grill looks too much like a greasy spoon, and drive right on by—that is, until you glanced at the parking lot—which is packed—or peeked in at the dining room—which is full. Once you're inside, you'll be pleasantly surprised by the crisp, clean decor: the woodgrain formica tables are well-spaced, the blue window frames a nice contrast with whitewashed walls, and even the green plants looking healthy and well-fed. A cheerful waitress will seat you with a smile, no matter how much sand you bring in from the beach, or whether everyone in your party has managed to come up with an even number of shoes.

Though you cut some corners for such reasonable prices, paper placemats and napkins—even paper cups—are a small price to pay for such excellent food and pleasant service. And the placemats with a drawing of a sugar plantation 'camp house' give hungry kids an opportunity to color, crayons courtesy of management. Another generous touch: sodas are served in a "bottomless cup" for $1.25, and the drinks are served immediately and refilled cheerfully. Better yet, try a milk shake ($1.75), which you can see and hear being made fresh at the gleaming silver fountain machine. No soft ice cream made pasty with thickener, Camp House Grill's shake has the genuine texture of ice cream mixed with milk. Mikey knows: it looks just like the "soup" he always makes in his bowl of ice cream! Camp House Grill makes kids feel welcome. Ten-and-unders can eat a "*menehune* special" cheeseburger or hot dog for only $2.25, while bigger little people can choose from junior burgers ($2.95 for 1/4 pound), fish, hot dogs, and four types of chicken breast sandwiches.

Everything is cooked to order, so you might have to wait a bit, but it will all seem worth while once you start eating. Waimea burger ($4.50), otherwise known as a barbecue cheeseburger, is perfectly cooked medium–rare with tangy sauce and great cheese. In a Hanapepe Burger, broiled pineapple and teriyaki sauce make an ideal complement to the beef, swiss cheese, lettuce, and tomato. Onion rings ($2.75) would steal the show if it weren't already long gone with the french fries. Barbecue chicken ($4.25/half) is sizzling hot and spicy, as are the pork ribs. To cool it all off, you can have draft beer, available by the glass, or pitcher for $6.75. Note: a different chef is in the kitchen for the dinner shift, so consistency may vary.

Camp House Grill is clean, cheerful, and sincere. What you see is what you get—and then some extras. A deer head and a stuffed rooster look out through the window at what is passing by on Rt 560. Don't let that be you!

On Rt 560 in Kalaheo. 332-9755 for take-out orders. Map: 2

Cantina Flamingo

As you turn the corner by the ocean, you may see a sign adorned with two pink flamingos. This tells you not only to turn left, but hints at the serendipity of the restaurant, which has become very successful for its generous portions at reasonable prices. A new owner has expanded the menu while keeping the most successful selections from the past.

Housed in the downstairs of a comfortable old home, this is one of the friendliest restaurants on Kauai. Servers come to the table as if glad to see you, and they fill your needs promptly. As soon as you are seated, a huge plate of chips arrives, accompanied by delicious salsa with the color and taste of fresh preparation: tomato chunks, slices of green onion and cilantro leaves. Prices are just as welcoming. Most items on the menu costs around $10, with *enchiladas, tacos,* and *burritos* less than $5.00, and dinner portions, served with rice and beans, are enormous. So are the margaritas, a house specialty, and you can choose from nine flavors, including such tropical delights as guava and coconut.

A house special, Mexican pizza ($6.95) is truly special, a large crisp tortilla generously topped with beans, cheese, green onions, olives and peppers (guacamole $.50 extra). *Nachos Flamingo* ($6.95) is another winner, served with beans and cheese and guacamole and green onion.

Entrees are generous. The *chimichanga* Kauai ($10.95), is outstanding— crispy, light, moist, and generously stuffed with tasty, tender chicken breast, broccoli and vegetables. Another good choice is the *burrito Juarez* ($9.95), a flour tortilla generously stuffed with still-pink slices of tender, juicy steak; mixed with avocado, salsa, and a delicious green tomatillo sauce; and smothered in melted cheese. *Fajitas* are served with so much sizzle that you automatically look up to see where the smoke alarms are located. The only disappointment was *Rellenos Pacifico* ($13.95), served with a cheese and wine sauce that seemed irrelevant to the fish and shrimp, which were unfortunately a bit dry.

You probably won't be able to finish everything, but waiters are helpful with carry-out containers, so you can plan on a lunch the following day. Some of our readers have found the spicing too bland, so if you like it hot, be sure to state your preference to the waiter! The some who don't like it hot can choose a half-pound hamburger ($6.95) or a plain hunk of sirloin ($9.95). No matter your taste preference, be sure to save room for dessert. Deep fried macadamia nut ice cream ($3.50) "rolled in a blend of honey, cinnamon, and oats" (which the waiter told us with a grin was Team Flakes) is delicious, and the Mexican flan ($2.50) is outstanding, a caramel topped custard with a perfectly soft and creamy texture.

Cantina Flamingo fills an important need on the south shore: an inexpensive, high-quality family Mexican restaurant in a tourist area known for pricey dining. The all-you-can-eat taco bar makes even group dining a reasonable proposition. Kids love it! They can make a *taco, tostada,* or *burrito* containing *exactly* the right combination of ingredients in *precisely* the correct proportion! Kids pay $6.95, adults $8.95 ($7.95 before 5:30 pm).

2301 Nalo Road in Poipu. Open daily 5-9:30 pm. No reservations. Taco Bar opens at 3:30 pm, 'Flamingo Hour'. 724-9505 for take out. Map: 3

Dondero's, Hyatt Regency Hotel

Decorated in vibrant green and white, Dondero's is an elegant restaurant, the showpiece of the lovely Hyatt Regency Hotel, which was designed to capture the more leisurely pace of the 1920's before jet-set timetables pushed life into permanent fast-forward. Dondero's dining room is beautiful, with tables attractively arranged on two levels and comfortably spaced for privacy. Gracefully twining ivy vines painted on the walls complement a striking design of rich jade green and white tiles, some patterned with seashells, so that the room seems poised on the edge of a seaside garden, with large windows and french doors opening to the terrace. At night, tables set with china and silver are softly lit by crystal lamps with pleated shades.

Surrounded by this elegance, as well as the strains of classical music, you consider a menu which offers a dozen *a la carte* entrees ranging in price from $21 (chicken with *porcini* mushrooms) to $26 (*Cioppino*). Pastas range from $9 to $12 and can also be ordered as full sized entrees ($16 to $22). Only two pastas are made fresh, however, while the rest are "imported."

Dinner begins with small loaves of delicious cheese bread, served with a deliciously spicy tomato pesto. Leek and potato soup ($4), tasty though not distinctive, was a better choice than a quite peppery minestrone, generous with tomatoes and squash. Spinach *tagliatelle* was served with a tomato sauce that was also quite spicy, but the waitress blandly took it back and returned with a substitute. You may find uncomplicated menu selections to be better choices than those which require finesse in seasoning.

Ono was perfectly grilled, tender, and tasty, but the "crust" of pine nuts and fennel was overly spicy. Fortunately, you could easily scrape it off and find the fresh fish flavorful underneath. The lamb was generous, four large chops which were tender but not very tasty. Fresh tomatoes and peppers and squash accompanied the entrees.

The wine list is expensive, with most selections more than $30 and only a dozen in the range of the $20's, including a Stratford Chardonnay at $28. You'll love the desserts— a smooth chocolate *mousse*, an outstanding *tiramisu,* as well as a strawberry *flambeau* with fresh vanilla ice cream.

At Dondero's, you should consider your dinner as a single course in your entire evening. For an aperitif, walk around the lovely hotel and then enjoy a cocktail or glass of wine in

'Stevenson's Library,' one of the most elegant bars anywhere, not only because of its gorgeous view, but also its design and appointments. You'll find tables for chess or checkers, even billiards, and best of all, comfortable couches for pleasant before-dinner conversation. After dinner, stroll the hotel's beautifully lit gardens and enjoy the breezes of the evening.

In the Hyatt Regency, Poipu. Credit cards. Valet parking. Children's menu 50% off selected items.

The House of Seafood

In the Poipu Kai Resort, the House of Seafood specializes in fresh fish, and because local fishermen are on good terms with the chef, you'll be able to choose from an amazing variety. This is a big advantage in winter months, when the surf can get very rough for the fishing boats. While other restaurants may have fresh fish in short supply and limited variety, the House of Seafood will probably be offering as many as eight or nine choices!

You'll also find a great variety in preparation, creations of the chef as he contemplates what has been hooked that day and decides how best to cook it. You might find fresh sea bass cooked in parchment, fresh *mahi mahi* sauteed with macadamia nuts, fresh snappers of every hue, or even shark. Entrees are accompanied by clam chowder or salad, a vegetable, and delicious herbed wild rice. But you won't want to pass up the appetizers: mushrooms stuffed with crab, or tangy deep fried artichokes.

Attention to detail makes each part of the meal enjoyable. Service is polite and friendly, and you get the feeling that the staff is genuinely interested in doing the job well. Homemade herb rolls and butter arrive with the entrees, the creation of a chef who likes to experiment. Your dinner will include a salad, attractively served on a glass plate with fanciful dressings, like a passion fruit vinaigrette and a tropical alternative to 'thousand island' made with guava and fresh basil. Or you may choose the seafood chowder instead, which is generous with fresh fish and shrimp, though thick rather than creamy.

You can count on your fish to be generous and perfectly cooked, and what makes House of Seafood such a special place is the variety of interesting preparations. One of the finest fresh fish we tasted anywhere, for example, was a fresh *ahi* flawlessly broiled and served 'luau style', with a light sauce delicately flavored with taro leaf and coconut. Wonderful! Also excellent was the sauteed fresh *mahi mahi* served with orange and cashew sauce. Or try the more pungent fresh *ehu*. *Hapu apu'u* or sea bass may be served with a delicious combination of teriyaki, orange, and *miso* sauce on a bed of soft noodles, or sometimes with a curry sauce that is too strong for its delicate flavor. *Paella* arrives as a huge platter, generous with clams, shrimp and fish. Entrees, which average around $20, are served with fresh vegetables, carefully cooked and attractively served, like cauliflower with a light and lemony cream sauce. If you're not sure you'll like the sauce on your fish, ask to have it served on the side, and be sure to ask for some of the chef's special tartar sauce with fresh pineapple.

You can spend a lovely evening in the comfortable, quiet dining room, tastefully decorated with rattan and lots of leafy plants. Most tables are near a window, are well spaced for privacy, and attractively set with green cloths and shining silver and glassware. On the well-selected wine list, you can find some good choices at reasonable prices, most priced in the mid 20's, like a Murphy-Goode Sauvignon Blanc for $22.

At House of Seafood, the personal touch is everywhere. On one of the best children's menus on the island, children can choose from steak ($7.75), hamburger ($5.50), fresh fish ($6.75) and wait until you hear this entree from a generous and thoughtful management—grilled cheese! Each full dinner includes soup or salad, rice or french fries, vegetable, dessert and a drink. Such recognition of children's real tastes is not surprising, for the chef has named his most special dessert after his own daughter. With great pride, your waiter will describe "Crepes Tiffany," available only when the kiwi fruit is at perfect ripeness. Or you can try excellent homebaked pies with flaky crusts, or coconut strudel with lots of shredded coconut.

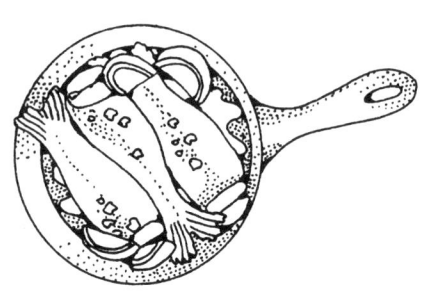

Come to the House of Seafood on a night with a moon. The dining room is open to the night air, and from the darkened room lit by the soft light of candles floating in bowls of flowers, you can watch the last light of evening fade, changing the pattern of darkness with each moment. Later as stars twinkle through thin filmy clouds, the full moon glows in the deep blue sky, while soft breezes rustle through the hibiscus leaves and crickets sing themselves to sleep.

In the Poipu Kai Resort. Credit Cards. 742-6433. Map: 3

Keoki's Paradise

At Keoki's you might feel as if you've wandered onto the set of Gilligan's island. The tables are arranged on several levels around a wandering lagoon, where taro grows among the lava rocks, and you can even spot a frog or two resting among the lily pads. Green plants hang everywhere, and the night is filled with the sound of crickets. The wood tables are roomy and the rattan chairs comfortably upholstered. Ask to be seated outside, where dining is cooled by evening breezes and you can watch the light of evening fade and the sky turn luminous with shining stars. Should a passing shower threaten to douse your table, waiters will quickly set up the awnings!

One of the most successful restaurants on the south shore, Keoki's offers reasonable prices as well as an atmosphere of South Pacific chic. Long lines of hungry diners begin to form at about 7 pm, so even with a reservation, expect company when you arrive!

To the right of the entrance is a bar and lounge, serving *pu pus*, nachos, and burgers, as well as Mexican specialties from a Seafood and Taco bar where you can watch the chef chop, saute, and stuff burritos. His stainless steel grill, he modestly claims, is 'clean enough for surgery!' Come early and grab one or the half dozen tables near the bar, and you can make an inexpensive dinner of these Mexican treats.

Keoki's main dining room features a reasonably priced, extensive menu offering fresh fish, chicken, steak (sirloin only) as well as a huge portion of prime rib ($19.95 "while it lasts"—so you might want to phone ahead and reserve a portion when you reserve your table!) The 16 ounce portion, though generous, is still 10 ounces less than the one that made Keoki's famous! But that 26 ounce portion is apparently available these days only during the "Sunset Special," from 5:30 to 6:15 pm ($17.95). On the regular menu, more than 20 dinner entrees include salad, rice, and fresh bread. Nine cost less than $10, and for about $6, children (even adults) can choose a burger or chicken sandwich. Children's full dinners are reasonable, $4.50 for a hamburger or $8.95 for chicken breast.

The Portuguese bean soup ($2.95) was generous though in need of more distinctive seasoning, but a better choice than the dinner salad, a sharply seasoned Caesar salad with too much cheese, too many croutons, and the limpness of bulk preparation. You might request plain Romaine lettuce with oil and vinegar! While the sourdough rolls seemed of the brown and serve variety, the homemade bran muffins were excellent. The wine arrived well–chilled, one of several reasonable choices for under $20.

The waiter recommended the fresh–baked *opakapaka* ($18.95), which was moist, delicately flavored, and fragrant with basil. The fresh *ahi* ($17.95) was moist and flaky. Fresh *ono* ($16.95), was flaky enough but a bit small and served with a strongly flavored wine and caper sauce which should have been left on the side. The prime rib ($19.95), truly enough for two, was moist and tender though a bit bland. Barbecued ribs were not as tasty as we expected because the sauce seemed added after rather than during the cooking process. A better choice is teriyaki sirloin, carefully marinated and very tender. Lobster tail ($17.95) was moist and tasty, though be sure to tell the kitchen to hold the paprika, for someone in there just loves to use that red dust! Herb rice and vegetables were adequate. Be sure to try the hula pie ($1.95), for which Keoki's is justly famous. The oreo crust holds macadamia nut ice cream topped with chocolate, whipped cream and macadamia nuts.

Keoki's attracts a large clientele because of reasonable prices and adequate cooking. Don't expect the kitchen to excel in subtle seasoning and you won't be disappointed. Simple dishes, like fresh fish plainly prepared, are the best. Keoki's is a good choice for the truly hungry, and for those who love the truly hokey, for you can giggle during dinner under those fake Polynesian torches about which Hollywood script you would most like to be acting out in Keoki's Paradise.

In the Kiahuna Shopping Village, Poipu. Credit cards. Reservations a must 742-7534. Coffee: $1. Dinner 5:30-10 pm nightly. Seafood & Taco Bar 4:30-midnight. Map: 3

The Koloa Broiler

The least expensive steak house on Kauai, the Koloa Broiler has devised a unique solution to the problem of overhead. Diners not only help themselves to salad, baked beans, and bread, but even cook their own entrees on an enormous indoor grill. A glass case at the entrance contains the menu in its raw form: mahi mahi ($8.45), barbecued chicken ($8.45), top sirloin ($9.45), beef kabob ($8.45), fresh fish ($9.95-$12.95) and a hamburger ($5.95). The waitress will bring your selection to you raw, recite a few cooking instructions, and then you're on your own, marking your cooking time by a huge clock positioned by the grill.

While this approach has obvious advantages, it is not foolproof. Hopping up and down to check the progress of your meal is hardly relaxing, and sometimes conversation distracts the attention you need for careful cooking. You end up being responsible for the quality of your dinner, so you can hardly send it back if it turns out raw or burnt. A few tips: you might try marinating your steak in the Italian salad dressing while you enjoy a cocktail. And despite instructions to the contrary, removing the foil wrapping from the chicken or fish in the final moments of cooking enhances the flavor. While your entree cooks, you can also toast some buttered bread.

The dining room is large and plain. Decorated with a few hanging plants and whirling ceiling fans, it has all the ambiance of a converted storeroom. And in certain spots, the fragrance of the grill is unmistakable. (This is one place where a non-smoking section is practically impossible!) But the real attraction here is unbeatable prices. It's a change of pace from the usual restaurant experience, and if you're on a tight budget, you won't find a more satisfying way to spend your evening or your money.

In the heart of Koloa. Reservations 742-9122. Map : 3 Credit cards. Children's dinner: hamburger or cheeseburger. Open for lunch and dinner, 11:00 am to 10:00 pm. Full bar.

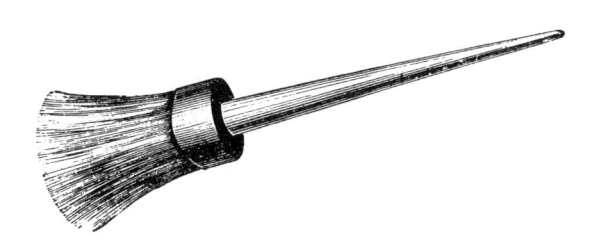

Naniwa

The Japanese restaurant in the Sheraton Poipu Hotel, Naniwa won't whisk you away to an exotic world. The cuisine may be Japanese, but the restaurant was clearly designed with western clientele in mind, so you won't have to remove your shoes upon entering, and you won't be sitting on the floor.

Naniwa serves some of the finest Japanese cuisine on the island. Try red *miso* soup ($2.50), a wonderfully delicate broth garnished with tiny mushrooms and bean curd, elegantly served in a covered bowl with green onions nestled in the top. Spectacular! So is the *sukiyaki*, a magnificent platter of thin sliced beef, *enoki* and *shiitake* mushrooms, napa cabbage, bean curd, onions, noodles, watercress, and carrots. Not only beautiful to look at, this dish is beautifully prepared at your table: the beef tender, the vegetables fresh and crisp, the sauce tasty and the total combination a wonderful balance of flavors.

Tableside cooking is expensive, about $22 per person, and a minimum of two must order the same dish. Besides *sukiyaki*, you can choose *yosenabe* (seafood and vegetables) *shabu shabu* (beef) and *uldonsuki* (seafood). If you can't agree to share, you can choose from three full-course Japanese dinners ($21.50 to $23.95) or from ten Japanese/American type entrees including chicken teriyaki ($16.50), fresh fish ($17.95), teriyaki N.Y. steak ($18.95) and lobster ($28.50). Those looking for a more reasonably priced meal can try *sushi*, available in beautiful arrays ($4.95 and up) or by the piece. Weeknights from 6-6:45 pm, you can have a complete dinner with soup or salad, rice, ice cream and tea for only $18, or try the 'all-you can-eat-buffet' on Saturdays ($21).

Naniwa's chef makes the dining experience worthwhile, though you may find dining noisier that you'd like in a room which, though attractive, is rather small and crowded. While the meals are elegantly presented and attractively arranged, you will eat them on paper placemats with disposable chopsticks. And though the restaurant overlooks a lovely garden and lagoon, the windows are not open to evening breezes. Most disappointing of all, the wine list is small and so undistinguished that Japanese beer may be your best bet!

But after all, it's what is on the table that counts. At Naniwa, what's comes to the table is worth the wait and the noise.

In the Sheraton Poipu Beach Hotel. Reservations a must; specify a window table, as they are slightly more private. Map: 3

Plantation Gardens

Set in several beautifully landscaped acres of specimen cactus and tropical flowers, Plantation Gardens is one of the most lovely and romantic restaurants on Kauai. The dining room and bar were originally the porches of a graceful old home, with soft evening breezes as delightful as the view, and you feel poised on the edge of the garden, with the mysterious shapes of the plantings dark against the star filled sky. Tables are spacious, with glasses and silver shining amid softly glowing candles and fresh flowers. Chairs are comfortable, and service is friendly, quiet, and leisurely, so that you can linger a long time over dinner and conversation.

The specialty remains seafood, and you will probably find, in addition to the usual *ahi* and *ono*, at least one other variety such as *uku*, albacore, *ulua*, broadbill, or *kahala*. On our most recent visit, the *ahi* ($17.95 for 8 oz) was superb, cleanly broiled so that it was perfectly moist and tender, with a flavor so wonderful that it seemed a shame to use the *teriyaki* sauce at all. The fresh sauteed *uku* ($18.95) was moist and flaky, served with a sweet, fruity sauce that was a nice counterpart, although once again, the fish was even more delicious by itself. Some sauces are worse than a distraction, however, like a salty sauce served with an otherwise excellent broiled fresh salmon, so take the precaution of having all sauces served on the side. Dinners include a tasty rice pilaf as well as a vegetable, in our case carrots with honey and tarragon.

An expanded menu emphasizes the flavors of the Pacific Rim. A new appetizer, grilled chicken salad, features lichees, red peppers, fried wontons, and a sweet and spicy dressing with cilantro and papaya ($9.95). Soups and salads are *a la carte*; spinach salad ($2.95) is usually excellent, or try the soup of the day, like a wonderful cream of fresh butternut squash soup ($2.95). With these extras, your dinner is going to be expensive, although five 'lite cafe suppers' are a more reasonably priced alternative, and include chicken breast teriyaki ($10.95) or a prime rib sandwich ($11.95) with vegetable and bread. A "garden menu" has been introduced, offering lower priced suppers served in the less formal patio adjacent to the cocktail lounge. The wine list still contains some good choices at reasonable prices. Half the California whites cost around $20, with an old stand-by like Robert Mondavi Fume Blanc priced at $22. Ours arrived not quite chilled, so order early and request an ice bucket!

Dinner at Plantation Gardens is going to be expensive, but you will probably remember the evening with pleasure, for the enchantment of the setting and the politeness of the service. Bring 'Off' in case mosquitoes like to pick on you, and bring your camera for spectacular garden pictures before dinner.

In the Kiahuna Resort, Poipu. Reserve a day or two in advance 742-1695. Specify a window table but be prepared to wait for it—as much as 20 minutes if the staff is not efficient! Credit cards. Children's dinner $7.95 (prime rib, chicken, fish). House wine: Robert Mondavi $6.50/$12.00. Coffee/brewed decaf $1.50. Map 3

Tamarind, Stouffer Waiohai Hotel

Tamarind was the first luxury, gourmet restaurant to open on Kauai, and at the time, some said it could never last! But Tamarind has proven how durable high quality can be over the years. It survived competition from Nobles at the Princeville Sheraton and then The Masters at the Westin and Midori at the Hilton, all of which have now closed, the victims of high cost and low profit. So Tamarind is once again alone in its class, offering consistently fine continental cuisine in a formally elegant setting.

The dining room is lovely, both formal and elegant, though you'll find no windows to let in fragrant evening breezes or offer glimpses of starry skies. Instead, the eye is drawn to the appointments of the room itself, the tables dressed in white linen, set with green and white china, shining glassware and a single bloom in a silver vase. Air-conditioned and plush, the room is hushed by thick carpet and linen tablecloths. Virtually the only sound you hear is the tinkle of glassware and silver to the strains of a piano in the adjacent lounge.

The evening begins with a basket of *lavosh*, served while you consider the menu, which includes a dozen entrees as well as a four course *prix fixe* dinner ($41), and an interesting range of appetizers. A splendidly smooth papaya bisque ($4.75) makes a spectacular appearance in a carved papaya, although some may find it overly sweet for an appetizer. Tahitian crab soup ($6.50) is mildly sweet and creamy, generous with crab and spinach. Lobster ravioli ($9) is also superb, three large pasta pillows perfectly cooked *al dente*, puffed with shellfish, and attractively presented in a tomato tarragon sauce.

One of the finest fresh fish creations on the island is the fresh *opakapaka* ($26.50) sauteed light, crispy and tender, served with a lime and macadamia nut sauce, though the chef's most special sauce, made with papaya and ginger, is available if you ask for it. The rack of lamb ($28.75) appeared as four chops, perfectly cooked and tender, with a piquant *poha* berry glaze. With the entrees arrived fresh beans, baby squash, and a ripe tomato stuffed with *shiitake* mushrooms.

Desserts are one of Tamarind's finest achievements. Chocolate *souffle* ($6) was perfectly light, yet rich in flavor. Also exceptional was the passion fruit *flan* ($3.50) in a flaky crust colorful with strawberry slices. Or try *profiteroles* filled with coconut custard, topped with ginger cream sauce!

Although now more limited as a result of a management decision, Tamarind's wine list is still outstanding. California wine-lovers will find most of the best vintners from Napa, Sonoma, Mendocino, or Central Coast, while those who prefer European wines will find many choices, as well as good variety in the medium price range. Wine steward Jeffrey can be extremely helpful in making a selection; ask him about special vintages not on the regular list.

By the end of the evening you will come to know the Jeffrey, the *maitre d'* and your waiter by their first names. The staff is attentive without hovering, and unfailingly pleasant. Each course is elaborately presented on china with silver domes topped with carved pineapples, and as each plate is removed, you are asked how you enjoyed what was on it. Every effort is made to make you —and not just your meal—the center of attention. From beginning to end, the dining experience is marked by an almost flawless attention to detail and by the chef's considerable expertise. Two will pay close to $100, including wine, and the evening will be so enjoyable that you will consider the money well spent.

In Poipu. 742-9511 for reservations, at least a day in advance. Map: 3

Taqueria Nortenos

When you drive by the Kukui'ula Center in Poipu, you often see a jammed parking lot and a small cluster of people on the sidewalk. This congestion is due to Taqueria Nortenos, which serves some of the best, most sensibly priced Mexican food on Kauai.

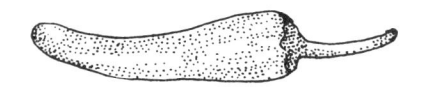

You'll have to wait on the take-out line by the tiny kitchen next door (There's even an express window), and while you're being driven crazy by the wonderful aromas, you can calculate the price of your selections. The menu offers meat or vegetarian *burritos, tacos, and tostadas* at modest prices ($2-$3) with fillings and toppings priced separately. If you worry about fat in your diet, you can skip the sour cream and not pay for it! Beans, rice, and sauce come free, and inexpensive extras like tomatoes or onions will be cooked right inside your *burrito* or *taco*. *Nachos* are generous with cheese and plenty of everything, and you'll find both fresh corn and flour chips. *Guacamole* is chunky with avocados. Your beef *burrito* will be filled with huge chunks of tender and tasty shredded beef, and covered with cheese, in a portion so large you will be hard pressed to clean your plastic plate. Spices are mild, with plenty of hot sauce available to please everyone's taste.

In the Kukuiula shopping center, on the road to Poipu. Mon-Sat 11 am till 11 pm. Wed 11 am till 5:30 pm. 742-7220. Map 3.

Waiohai Terrace

One of the best kept secrets on the south shore is lunch at the Waiohai Terrace. Not only are prices surprisingly reasonable, but The Terrace is the prettiest dining spot on the south shore, with tables only a few steps from the sea. As the waves sparkle in the sunshine, you can watch surfers hunting the perfect ride, or listen to occasional rainshowers dance among the flowers. Food is delicious, and service could not be more friendly.

We arrived one afternoon hungry and sandy from the beach, not in the mood to be patient. To give you an idea, when the breadbasket arrived, all four buns disappeared before the basket came to rest on the tabletop. The good natured waitress, clearly a mother herself, immediately whisked the basket away with promises of a speedy refill.

Lunch entrees were excellent. The chicken salad pleased our almost-vegetarian Mirah, who loved the dressing and found the chicken suitably free from skin and other impurities. The reuben was so tasty that Jeremy refused to keep his bargain and share. The cobb salad was enormous, filled with wonderful vegetables and meats. The club sandwich, especially tailored to Mikey's specifications, presented the perfect balance of flavors and was devoured to the last crumb. Lauren loved her hamburger, and all four children were all smiles by the time the bill arrived. When a family of six can dine next to the ocean for only $40, that's almost as remarkable as the fact that the rain, which had been pouring down as were seated, was cleared away along with our plates, making lunch at the Waiohai a perfect way to spend an afternoon shower!

The Terrace is also one of our family's favorite breakfast spots, and a tried and true location for 'Special Mornings with Daddy.' The breakfast buffet (available only when the hotel is full, so call ahead) is almost a lovely as the beachfront setting. For only $6 for children and $13.50 for adults, you can feast in a spectacular, peaceful spot. Kids will love to hand-pick an assortment of fruits, pastries and eggs, take a few bites, then trade in their plates and start all over again— as you try to look the other way! Even menu service is reasonably priced. Service is kind, compassionate, and friendly.

In the Stouffer Waiohai Resort Hotel, Poipu Beach. Credit cards. Map 3.

Flank Steak Lae Nani

Marinade: 1/4 cup honey or sugar, 1/3 cup hot water, 1/3 cup soy sauce, 2 tbsp oil, 1 clove garlic, 1 star anise or 1 thick slice fresh ginger.

Marinate at least 48 hours in the fridge, grill steak over coals or saute it in a pan. Slice across the grain in thin slices, angled about 45 degrees. The star anise, available dry in oriental graocery markets, gives the steak a unique, superb flavor, a delicate touch of licorice!

Tropical Chicken Salad

Mix together chopped nuts, apple chunks, chicken chunks, diced celery and carrots in quanitites you like, along with enough mayonnaise to blend. Add 1/2 to 1 tsp curry. Let stand 1/2 hour.

Garnish with sliced bananas and chopped m acadamia nuts. Serve on a bed of manoa lettuce. Dressing: blend 1/2 cup mashed ripe banana with 1/2 cup mayonnaise, salt, pepper and juice of 1/2 fresh lemon.

Waiohai Sunday Champagne Brunch

Sunday Brunch at the Waiohai has become, over the years, justly famous among local people as a truly magnificent feed. No ordinary affair of warmed over eggs and sausage, this buffet features five tables laden with a baroque display of meats, seafood, salads, fruits and pastries of every description. Each platter delights the eye with a colorful pattern of food ingeniously carved, sliced, sculptured, garnished, twisted, even disguised as flowers or birds. You will find *sashimi*, not only *ahi* but whole *ehu* (red snapper), sliced in an intricate criss-cross pattern from head to tail as well as octopus and shrimp (still in the shell), *terrines* and *pates*, salads and fresh vegetables, fruits and juices, croissants, cheese cakes, and pies of every flavor. Waffles come with whipped medallions of strawberry or banana butter. Before your eyes you can have an omelette created with your choice of fillings, a pasta tossed with marinara or cream sauce, or juicy roast beef sliced to your plate by a smiling attendant. As the morning wanes, the food selection changes, so even if your appetite flags under all this exercise, you might be tempted by some new confection just whisked out from the kitchen.

Even in this culinary Eden, however, there is a snake—in this case the winding line you must wait on for at least a half hour no matter when you join it. The line begins to form at 9 am. Since the dining room fills rapidly when the doors open at 10 am, arriving at line's end after 9:30 will probably condemn you to waiting until some of the first sitting retire from the field. That can take an hour, so arrive early, bring the paper, and enjoy some complimentary coffee while you make the acquaintance of those around you on line. The hostess suggests a 1:30 pm arrival for the shortest wait. The best solution: find friends to make a party of ten (that earns you a reservation) and call two days in advance. Just keep your fingers crossed as you walk past the line of hungry people not-so-patiently awaiting their turn ($25/adults).

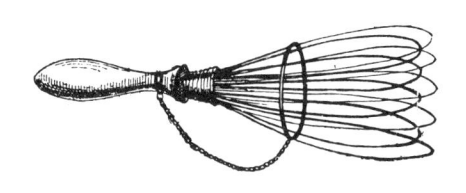

Westside Restaurants

All Kine Burgers

For years, the Windward Diner hugged the side of the road in Hanapepe. Then Suzy breezed in from Watsonville, California to take over the mini-kitchen. At first, she turned out terrific vegetarian sandwiches and health food creations. But health food does not apparently have a large following on this part of Kauai, and so Suzy switched her menu to something with more universal appeal— hamburgers.

In our opinion, the hamburger menu is, unfortunately, not nearly as special. The patties are neither particularly generous nor especially tasty. The basic patty, which is fairly thin, costs $2 (either at breakfast or at lunch), with additions like lettuce, tomato, cheese, or guacamole priced at 3/$1. The Vegetarian burger ($4) turned out to be a surprisingly tasty concoction of grains. French fries ($1.25) can be a bit on the dry side, but onion rings ($2) are excellent.

Dining is spartan, so don't look for amenities (This is after all, a diner). Your orders are served on sheets of wax paper on five tiny tables. French fries arrive in paper bags with envelopes of catsup. Summertime temperatures can rise quickly in the tight quarters, despite the efforts of two ceiling fans. Use the take-out window and pack your food up to go to the beach!

The hamburgers are not special, but on the other hand, prices are low and on this side of the island you won't find a McDonald's or a Burger King—yet! For $2, you can get a good deal on a hamburger from Suzy. And if you don't expect more than fast food, you probably won't be disappointed.

In Hanapepe on Rt 50, just west of the Green Garden Restaurant.

The Green Garden

There has been a Green Garden Restaurant for about as long as Kauai has been called the Garden Island. A local legend, it has been owned and operated by the same family since 1948, its reputation based on generous portions and inexpensive prices. The menu features American, Japanese, and Chinese dinners, many priced below $5. Even at lunch the meals include several courses as well as a beverage. Service is fast and very friendly at the long, ranch style tables, and although the dining room may look and sound more like a high school cafeteria than a garden, you certainly get full value for your money. Where else could you find a hamburger platter with fries, a salad, dessert, and iced tea for under $4? At $5.50, the fresh *ulua* tempura or shrimp *tempura* are also bargains. For children, club sandwiches are about $4, and grilled cheese only $1.95—remember: this price includes salads plain enough for picky eaters, lots of fries and a drink!

The pies, though, would stand out at any price, and we recommend them all—the chocolate cream pie is a child's favorite treat, and the coconut cream pie has a light flaky crust filled with marvelously light egg custard topped with toasted coconut. The macadamia nut cream pie is equally delicious. The *lillikoi* chiffon pie, for which the Green Garden is justifiably famous, has the lightest texture imaginable and a taste of passion fruit that will arouse your taste buds.

Try to avoid arriving at noon, when tour buses frequently pull into the lot. But even if you're caught in the lunchtime crush, your service will not suffer because this staff has group service down to a science. Granted that food quality is affected by the high volume, and that the pace is a bit hectic, the Green Garden is terrific for large families on small budgets. Children are treated with tolerance, and when parents give up efforts to make them sit still at the table, youngsters can play with the video games on the enclosed porch. The Green Garden also serves dinner, with most of the same entrees priced about $1 higher than lunch.

On Rt 50 in Hanapepe. Reservations suggested for dinner. 335-5422. Breakfast 7 am-11 am. Lunch 11 am-2 pm. Dinner 5 pm-8:30 pm. Closed Tuesday nights. Credit cards. Map: 2

Toi's Thai Kitchen

You can't get more underground that Toi's Thai Kitchen! You dine in what could be described as a large carport connecting two buildings, one of them a sleepy looking bar called 'Traveler's Den.' Around you are a half dozen formica dinette sets, some accompanied by card table chairs, and beneath your feet is linoleum whose pattern, nondescript to begin with, has long since worn away. Off to the side, a television set on the counter may be showing an old black and white movie of the same vintage as the painted cinderblock walls. A few plants try, and fail, to liven up the decor. If you were striving to be tactful, you could say that this dining room is unpretentious and clean.

No matter the appearance of the dining room, what comes down the steps from the kitchen door is nothing short of spectacular. Toi's homegrown business, begun about three years ago, has developed a loyal clientele of former disbelievers who have spread the word, attracting more people who can't believe their eyes when they arrive — and shake their heads when they leave.

We arrived for lunch one afternoon, hungry and sandy from the beach. After a brief look, we might have turned right around if it were not too late to go anywhere else! As the only customers, we were soon made to feel welcome, receiving swift and friendly service from Toi and her young daughter. After taking our order, Toi disappeared up the steps again and all we heard was sizzle and whoosh. Then, one by one, dishes with magical aromas began to arrive at our table— spring rolls meltingly crisp, served with fresh lettuce, mint leaves, and a zesty peanut sauce ($5.95). Special Thai saimin ($4.95) arrived next, a marvel of color and taste! Fresh white flat noodles float in a gently spiced broth colorful with vegetables, several varieties of bean sprouts, and lots of tender chicken. Everyone loved it, and only the strictest self-control kept us from immediately ordering bowls all around!

Lunch includes a small salad of shredded cucumber, carrots, tomatoes, served on fresh manoa lettuce with a tasty sweet vinegar dressing, topped with ground peanuts. This cool interlude was followed by a hot yellow curry that pleased Jeremy, our spice specialist, who loved the flavor and the generous portion of tender chicken and potatoes (the other option for green, red, or yellow curries is eggplant). Pad Thai ($6.95) was another wonderful dish, the tender chicken and fresh Thai noodles sweetened with coconut milk and fresh basil. Fresh eggplant sauteed with tofu and huge fresh mushrooms was a marvelous contrast, both pungent and spicy ($5.95). Thai fried rice ($5.95) was everyone's favorite, so colorful and tasty that it was devoured to the last grain.

After a hard morning on the beach, this is a perfect place to get a fresh start on the afternoon. We were astounded to find that our hungry family of six could enjoy such a feast for less than $40, and at dinner, entrees are priced only about a dollar more than at lunch. If mosquitoes like to pick on you, bring along some "Off!" You won't find Toi's Thai Kitchen listed in the yellow pages (or even in the white pages), and the tiny sign is pretty hard to see. Part of the fun, however, is the adventure of the hunt! If you get lost wandering the streets of Kekaha, just look for the American flag. It'll be in the parking lot of the Post Office, which is next to the Traveler's Den, which is right in front of Toi's!

8240 Kekaha Road in Kekaha. Lunch 11-2:30 except Wednesdays and Saturdays. Dinner 5:30-8:30 pm except Saturdays. 337-9922

Kalaheo Steak House

For two years, the Kalaheo Steak House has been serving some of the best, most reasonably priced steaks on Kauai. The knotty pine interior is both pleasant and informal, so you will feel comfortable no matter what you are wearing. Plants divide the dining area into two sections, with comfortable booths along the wall and roomy tables in the middle. Fresh flowers and candles create a cozy, even romantic atmosphere.

The restaurant prides itself on the finest of ingredients. Steaks are top-grade midwestern beef. Bread is baked each day at the bakery across the street. Even the dinner salad is exceptional, served on a lovely glass plate with ripe tomatoes, white beans and red onions. Choose between a delicious papaya seed dressing, or as a special treat for cheese lovers, a blue cheese dressing made with the genuine article crumbled in a delicious vinaigrette and topped with fresh ground pepper.

The menu offers steaks, seafood, and poultry dinners which include rice or baked potato as well as the salad. Our waitress recommended the New York steak and the fresh ono, and we were pleased with both suggestions. The generous portion of ono was flaky and tender, though you might take the precaution of having the butter sauce served on the side, unless you love garlic. When the steak arrived too well done to be 'medium rare,' the replacement steak was even larger, perfectly cooked, and accompanied by a second baked potato— a steak well worth the wait!

Service is friendly and efficient, and prices are reasonable. The wine list is limited, pretty much, to Robert Mondavi, with the Woodbridge vintage cabernet sauvignon or sauvignon blanc served as the house choices for $10.50. Or you can have Miller on draft, served from the bar which occupies the front of the building.

You'll have an enjoyable, reasonably priced meal at the Kalaheo Steak House. If you are staying in Poipu, it's an excellent alternative to high priced hotel food, and if you are staying on the eastern shore, it's well worth the drive.

In Kalaheo. Credit Cards. Coffee .95

Wrangler's Restaurant

From the time you step across the wood plank floor into what looks like the set for that unfilmed Gunsmoke episode where Matt Dillon finally proposes to Kitty over a thick, juicy steak, you know that at Wrangler's, size is important. Everything is large. French fries come heaping on the plate. Seafood salad is a huge mound of crab, shrimp, scallops, olives and tomatoes. The "Wrangler Burger" fills the plate, and like the six other types of half-pound hamburgers includes soup or salad, as well as chips and salsa or french fries. The menu itself is enormous. You'll find Mexican dishes, plate lunches, sandwiches, and steaks, as well as Korean ribs and teriyaki. At dinner, you can choose from 9 steaks, including a 20 ounce sirloin or T-bone, 12 seafood and 7 Mexican dinners. And for all this size, prices are reasonable, starting at $5.75 for a hamburger steak dinner.

This menu fits the theme of big steers and hearty appetites. The dining room has a deliberately straightforward look, with old tools and saddles hung on the white-washed wood walls, as if to foster your belief that only the guys in the white hats eat here. Blue vinyl tablecloths and gingham curtains fit right in with the theme of square meals and honest deals. Juke boxes with titles from thirty years ago sit silent, waiting, perhaps, for a 1950's quarter to make them come to life.

Quantity seems more important than quality. The Mexican food is tasty, but the meat could be better trimmed. Soup is served in a big bowl, but the seasoning is hasty and overly salty. Ribs with *kim chee* could have been less fatty. Chicken was crispy and moist, but the overly salty *teriyaki* sauce should be left on the side, if not in the kitchen! The generous *ono* filet tasted somewhat bitter from the grill, and the brown mushroom sauce which fortunately was confined in a small bowl, helped the otherwise tasteless white rice much more the fish! The best bet is the hamburger, perfectly cooked, and served with lettuce and tomato on a soft kaiser roll.

Perched on the main street of sleepy Waimea in the historic AKO Building, Wrangler's attracts the local crowd. Order carefully, and Wrangler's can work for those exploring the island's westside, where there are few other choices for provisions.

Rt 50 in Waimea. Credit cards. Beer, wine, cocktails. Mon-Thurs 10:30 am to 9 pm; on Fri and Sat until 10 pm. 338-1218. No non-smoking section. Map: 2

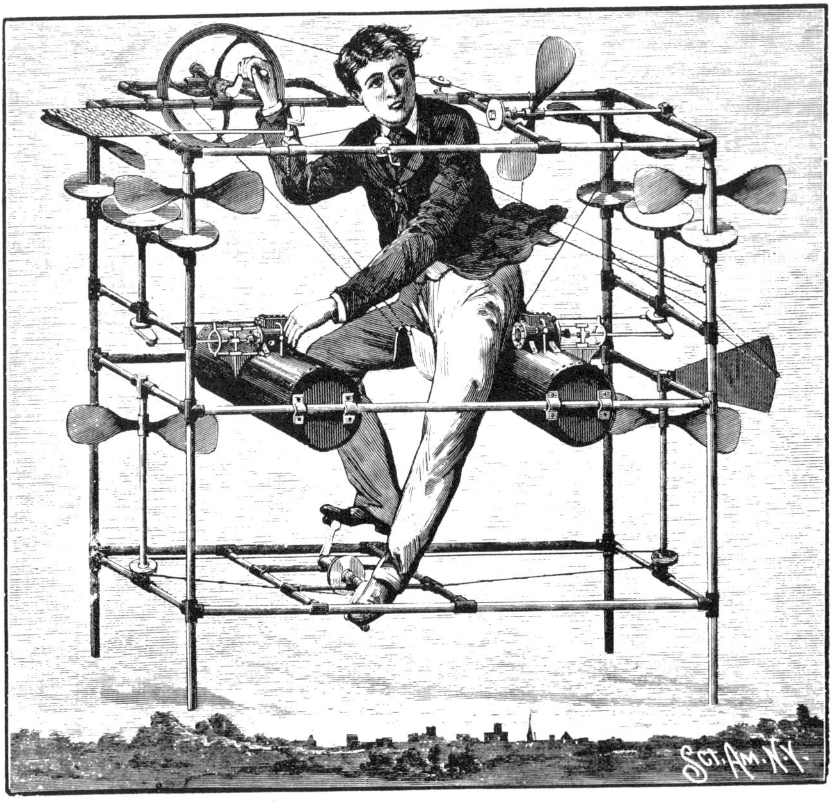
SCI. AM. N.Y.

Exploring Kauai

Helicoptering Kauai, 154
Boat Tours, 158
Museums & Special Tours, 162
Hiking & Camping, 165
Riding & Running, 168
Hawaiian Entertainment, 169
Golf, 168
Island Tastes, 170
Kauai Specialties, 173
Flower Leis, 174
Shopping, 175
Children's Corner, 179
Special Mornings with Daddy, 181
Travel Tips, 182
Traffic Hints, 186
Suggestions from our readers, 187
Restaurant Index, 188
Index, 190

Helicoptering Kauai

Many of the most beautiful places on Kauai are inaccessible by car. For this reason, a helicopter tour is an unforgettable way to see this spectacular island. Kauai is breathtakingly beautiful from the air, almost like an America in miniature, with rolling hills and valleys on the east coast and majestic mountains on the west. The island has a flat, dry southland as well as a forested wilderness to the north, and, on the west coast, wide sandy beaches where the setting sun paints the sky with gold before slipping silently into the enormous sea. There is even a "Grand Canyon" on a small scale, where pink and purple cliffs, etched by centuries of wind and rain into giant towers, seem like remnants of a lost civilization. So much variety is amazing on an island only 30 miles in diameter!

And what you'll see is beyond your fantasies—a mountain goat poised for an instant in a ravine, a white bird gliding against the dark green cliffs, a sudden rainbow in the mist, incredible, tower-like mountains of pink and brown in the Waimea "Grand Canyon," a glistening waterfall hanging like a slender silver ribbon through trees and rocks, a curve of pure white sand at the base of the purple and gold Na Pali cliffs, a spray of shining white foam bursting upon the rocky coast. Then, like the unveiling of the island's final mystery, the entrance into the very center of Mt. Waialeale's crater, where in the dimly lit mists of the rainiest place on the earth, waterfalls are born from ever falling showers. You have journeyed to the very heart of the island, the place of its own birth from the volcano's eruption centuries ago. From your hotel room, you would never have believed that all this splendor existed, and your only regret will be that you didn't take more film.

It's so special, you yearn to go up again. Even the second time, the tour is exhilarating. In fact, with a better sense of the island's geography, you are more sensitive to details too easily missed when you are overcome by the majesty of the scene for the first time. Perhaps you'll see some of the amazing irrigation canals and tunnels carved into the mountains a century ago to bring water to the sugar cane fields below. Or, on some remote and rocky precipice, a banana plant somehow thriving, all the more incredible because banana plants cannot grow from seed and must have somehow been planted there by the Hawaiians—generations before the arrival of helicopters!

Of the many companies offering tours, Jack Harter Helicopters stands out as special. Jack Harter is the most experienced pilot around, having offered the first air tour on Kauai more than 25 years ago. A local legend, he is the pilot most often called upon for help in emergencies. His flights are about an hour and a half, the best value for your money, and his pace is slow enough to offer a good look at the island's remote terrain. As he pilots his Bell Jet Ranger with skill and finesse, as smoothly as a dandelion seed in almost any weather, he makes sure that each passenger with a camera has a chance at the 'great shots' which can happen at almost every moment.

Jack's enormous knowledge is enough to make his tour memorable. Throughout the flight, he talks non-stop about the island he clearly loves, telling its legends and history, describing its plants and animals, reflecting on its politics and problems, and arguing the need for conservation and planned development. Helicopters seem to be more than just a business to him, and several Division of Forestry botanists doing research in a remote rainforest, or telephone workers repairing cables on an isolated mountain top, have told stories of receiving a miraculous "drop" of pizza, pot roast, and beer from a helicopter appearing out of nowhere!

Because of the expense of the tour, we worried about picking the "perfect day." That proved unnecessary. We began on what seemed in Lihue to be only a partly sunny day, but once in the air, we realized that the clouds would be above us rather than in our way and even enhanced the island's beauty with changing patterns of light. If the weather is too poor for a satisfying flight, Jack's policy is to cancel the trip. And even if you have already set out and he decides it is wiser to return, he will refund your money.

Jack Harter flies only three tours a day, so if you're a planner, write ahead (PO Box 306, Lihue HI 96766); if you wait till you're on the island, chances are you won't get on. Otherwise, we recommend interviewing several companies by asking specific questions (see 'Helicopter Tours & Safety' pp. 156-158) before making your choice.

One first-rate company is Will Squyres Helicopters, widely respected for its owner's good judgment and meticulous maintenance. You will have to specifically request Will's flight, however, for he flies only one or two days a week. His tour lasts just about an hour, and he offers a lively commentary on Kauai's colorful past and present, rather than the taped music used in many tours.

Looking at our slides and movies back home almost brings back the magic of that hour, when we seemed suspended in a horizon so vast as to seem limitless, and any effort to confine it within camera range was impossible. It is always the best day of the trip!

Helicopter Tours & Safety

Helicopter tours are big business. New companies keep entering the market, and intense competition has developed. Many people on Kauai feel that there is a wide variation in quality and safety, however. We have heard disquieting reports: some companies speed up tours in order to cut costs and squeeze as many tours into the day as possible. Some are plagued with high turnover in pilots who may have sufficient flying hours to be licensed but limited experience over Kauai's unique wilderness terrain.

With pilots from a dozen companies crowding the skies, safety is becoming an increasingly important issue, and you should do your homework carefully before making a choice. Accidents have happened. In June 1991, an Island Helicopters helicopter returning from a scenic tour piloted by Rick Shaw, crashed at the Lihue airport. The National Transportation Safety Board's initial report, quoted in the *Garden Island* February 5, 1992, stated that 'no fuel was present in the fuel tank', although NTSB's final determination of the probable cause of the crash is still pending as we go to press.

In recent years, the Federal Aviation Administration has investigated a number of companies conducting helicopter tours on Kauai, and will provide this information to citizens upon request. In May, 1989, one of the largest companies, Papillon Helicopters, settled a civil penalty action brought against it by the Federal Aviation Administration with a payment of $23,750. The FAA charged the company with violations of maintenance and pilot training. In July, 1990, Island Helicopters agreed to settle a civil penalty action brought against it by the FAA by the payment of $20,000. The FAA charged the company with violations of pilot training, record-keeping, and maintenance regulations. The company claimed that the settlement was not an admission of wrongdoing and contended that "none of the alleged discrepancies rendered the aircraft unairworthy." When we last queried the FAA computer in February, 1992, three helicopter companies were under investigation for violations

These are some key questions to ask when you are interviewing companies. First, find out whether the company is operating under a certificate issued by the Federal Aviation Administration under Part 135 of Federal Aviation Regulations. In order to maintain a certificate of this type, the company must follow a more rigorous (thus more expensive) maintenance program, and its pilots must pass annual flight tests not required of companies operating under Part 91 of Federal Aviation Regulations. This certificate must be displayed in the company's office. Ask to see it! Or check ahead of time by phoning the Federal Aviation Administration in Honolulu between 7:30 am and 4 pm Monday through Friday at (808) 836-0615. Ask an Operations Inspector whether the company you are considering is currently certificated under Part 135 of Federal Aviation Regulations. The distinction between Part 91 and Part 135 operators can tell you about the standards a company operates under, although this information is no guarantee of a company's performance when you're in the aircraft.

    The second question to ask is the exact length of the tour. Actual in-flight time for the around-the-island tour should be no less than 55 minutes, or Kauai will appear to whiz past your window! Even a 55-minute tour limits your opportunities to explore up-close the more remote terrain inside the island's perimeter, or to take satisfying pictures. But don't take the company's word for it. Ask for the daily flight schedule, subtract 5 minutes for landing and changing passengers, and draw your own conclusions!

    Beware of the advertisements—they can be very misleading. An ad which hypes the number of flying hours logged by the company's owner tells you nothing about the flying experience of his pilot employees. Ask who *your* pilot will be. Not every pilot employee who qualifies for a helicopter license has had extensive experience with Kauai's wilderness terrain. You also have a right to know whether the company, or *your* pilot, has been involved in any accidents during the past three years. Beware of companies which are reluctant to provide specific answers, or which say they "can't be sure" who will be piloting your flight. Call another company!

Don't take at face value the advertisements which claim that the owner is the "operator." Any owner can "operate" his company without being the pilot for every flight. That may be true of some flights—from one a day to one a month—but very possibly not true of your flight! You should also ask if the company's FAA certificate has ever been revoked or suspended, or if it is currently under FAA investigation for violations. And since each helicopter must display its individual 'certificate of airworthiness,' look for it or ask to see it.

The type of aircraft you will be flying is another consideration. The Bell Jet-Ranger seats one passenger in front and three in back. Some have rear windows that can be opened for fresh air, which prevents fogging. These back seats next to windows which can be opened are best for photographing. In the co-pilot's seat, you look down through the glass under your feet as if you were floating in a bubble. The Hughes 500-D helicopter seats two passengers in the rear and two in front next to the pilot. Like a large glass bubble, it has no windows to open. The A-Star helicopter is like a tour bus, seating 6 passengers—2 next to the pilot in front and 4 in the rear, with the center rear seats having a more limited view.

You should also ask about the cancellation policy in case of bad weather. Even in a rainstorm, we often see the choppers flying!

Find out whether you can get your money back if you're not very comfortable — or if you can't see very much — once you're in the air!

Boat Tours

The spectacular cliffs of the Na Pali coast are off limits to most visitors—unless they dare to hike on narrow and slippery trails or explore these steep and jagged ridges from a helicopter. Coastal boat tours are becoming an increasingly popular way to see at least some of these amazing cliffs up close. In fact, on a clear summer's day, Hanalei Bay is busy with an assortment of large and small launches, catamarans, and inflatable 'zodiacs' loaded with tourists either on their way out or coming back in!

At about half the price of a helicopter tour, boat tours are a more affordable alternative and, to some people, a lot more fun. Boats offer rough and ready adventure, particularly the zodiacs originally made popular for white water river rafting. In a calm ocean, the zodiacs can carry passengers right up to touching distance of the incredible cliffs, so close you can see water from mountain springs trickle through the rocky ridges and drop in shining ribbons to the sea. You can trace the patterns made over centuries by mineral deposits, or chronicle the island's history in lines of lava. You can explore caves etched into the cliffs, watch waterfalls sparkle in the sunshine, and marvel at how tenaciously plants and trees can cling to inhospitable rock. Dolphins may leap in arcs around you, so friendly they seem to be seeking companions in these strange looking black boats decked with brightly colored tourists.

Spectacular and romantic, boat tours are also big business. More than thirty companies are licensed on Kauai, offering half and full-day tours costing upwards of $65 per person. Because these companies compete so aggressively, many people on Kauai worry about safety: some companies run tours in marginal weather; others cram their boats to the maximum.

As a general rule, tours are the safest from May until October when the ocean is usually flat off the Na Pali coast. But the weather becomes much more unpredictable after winter storms begin in late October. Because winter surf can reach twenty feet in Hanalei Bay, sailboats and small craft are actually moved out of Hanalei to more protected Nawiliwili harbor on the island's southeastern leeward shore. Even after the small craft leave Hanalei for the winter, however, some companies still offer Na Pali coast boat tours. And although the companies will assure you that they run Na Pali tours only in safe weather, part of what makes the north shore so dangerous in winter is the unpredictability of the winds and the ocean swell. Winds can shift in twenty minutes, and so predicting surf conditions for up to six hours ahead can be tricky business!

Even on the best of summer days, the trip out along the Na Pali coast is a lot smoother than the return trip, when you ride into the wind and the water is more choppy. If the captain tells you the trip will be "wet and wild," he means the boat will be rolling up and down the swells, smacking into them with bursts of spray, definitely not a good idea for someone with a bad back! The return trip has been described as "riding the bull," and some adventurers even choose to sit astride the boat's inflated sides, although dangling legs are fair game for any Portuguese men o' war who happen to be floating by.

Because winter weather can be so chancy, you should pay careful attention to the company's cancellation policy. Many companies will charge you between 20% and 50% of the tour price if you cancel less than 24 hours in advance, and the company can collect this cancellation charge because they will probably take your credit card imprint as a way of confirming your reservation when you make it. Be forewarned: this policy leaves you little option if you don't feel comfortable with the look of the sky or the ocean on the morning of your tour. You may end up being charged if the company decides to send out the boats, even if your own assessment of the weather has made you decide not to be on board!

Boat traffic is another safety problem. You can see the results at Tunnels Beach, for example, long a favorite spot for north shore snorkeling. Because it's also the departure point for Captain Zodiac boat tours, you have to watch out for the boats as well as the fish when you're in the water! Boats and people have to share the only sandy channel out into the reef, and sometimes boat personnel can be overzealous in trying to keep swimmers out of the channel when boats are coming in or going out. Just remember: people, not boats, have the right of way!

All other boat company tours leave from Hanalei Bay. The sheer number of tours makes the departure point look like the first day of summer camp, so don't expect a lot of personal attention. The chiefs of each company bustle about, lists in hand, marshalling their groups, calling roll, and assigning people to boats which are pulled in for boarding like waiting schoolbuses, a time–consuming process, and annoying if you have to wait for the inevitable stragglers to show up.

Once out of Hanalei Bay, the view of the coast is spectacular, from the Haena reefs to Ke'e Beach, and then beyond to the cliffs where you and the porpoises share the same view of the craggy rock formations, the caves etched into sheer cliff, and the magnificent colors of sea and sky, the changing light of sun and shadow. When you ride into the caves, you plunge into a cold, wet world where the water sloshes eerily against the rocks, making you grateful to return to sunlight again. In one cave, the sunlight streams in through a giant hole in the ceiling, and a waterfall plunges in shining streams of sparkling drops.

At Hanako'a, the landscape changes from the dark, rich green of Hanalei to the reds and browns of the west, where vegetation is more sparse. While rainfall at Ke'e Beach measures nearly 125 inches a year, at Polihale on the westernmost end of the cliffs, it is only 20 inches.

Most tours include a stop for snorkeling and snacking, usually at Nu'alolo Kai, a calm spot with a protective reef where you can see hundreds of colorful fish. If you don't enjoy snorkeling, however, or if the weather is not cooperative, this stop is a waste of time. If it's sunny, beware of a burn! Bring plenty of sunscreen, and perhaps a hat and sunglasses to protect against the glare. For the return trip, which will be much more choppy, you might bring towels and dry clothes in a plastic bag. As the boat slaps head on into the waves, the salt spray can douse everything in the boat, including you and your camera! Some companies offer a power cruiser ride back. It's certainly more comfortable, but as far as view goes, it's like looking through the window of a tour bus! And despite the relative protection from the swell, some travelers still get seasick.
   Different craft will give you a different ride and a different experience of the coast line. Power boats are more comfortable than the rubber zodiacs, but they cannot hug the cliffs like the zodiacs, and the larger ones can't go into the caves. A compromise may be the small power catamarans, which are agile enough to go into the larger caves, and yet able to cut through the swell rather than riding up and over it. In winter, you might consider a south shore tour , which may be less spectacular but safer and more comfortable.
   Before you choose your tour, call several companies. Find out about the expected weather and surf conditions, and ask about the company's cancellation policy. You can also for 245-6001 for the weather report. Compare the coast guard-rated capacity of the craft with the number of passengers the company usually takes on board, keeping in mind that the more crowded the boat, the less comfortable you may be. Ask about your captain's experience; although every captain has to be coast guard licensed, some have more experience than others! And look carefully at discount coupons. One company, for example, offered a coupon for a $30 discount off a list price of $90. However, the same tour averaged about $65 at activity centers around the island, and just about no one ever paid the list price! And ask if you can save money by booking directly with the company rather than through an agent.

Museums and Special Tours

The story of Kauai is in many ways the story of the sugar plantations which shaped the island's multi-ethnic culture as much as its agriculture and economy, For this reason, a visit to the **Grove Farm Homestead** in Lihue offers a fascinating glimpse into the island's past. One of the earliest Hawaiian sugar plantations, Grove Farm was founded in 1864 by George Wilcox, the son of Protestant missionary teachers at Waioli Mission in Hanalei. Planting and harvesting Grove Farm's sugar crop, which grew from 80 acres to more than 1000, ultimately involved a workforce of several hundred Hawaiians, Chinese, Koreans, Germans, Portuguese, and Filipino laborers, who brought to Kauai a rich heritage of ethnic cultures. A two-hour tour takes you through Grove Farm's cluster of buildings nestled amid tropical gardens, orchards, and rolling lawns, but be warned: the tour is extremely popular and you'll need to reserve a place at least a week in advance. You'll see the gracious old Wilcox home, the large rooms cooled by breezes from shaded verandas, and elegantly furnished with oriental carpets, magnificent koa wood floors and wainscotting, and hand crafted furniture of native woods. You will also tour the "board and batten" cottage of the plantation housekeeper, who came to Kauai, like many Japanese women, as a "picture bride" for a laborer too poor to travel home to select his wife in person. All buildings are covered by traditional "beach sand paint" (literally sand thrown against wet paint) to protect them against both heat and damp for as long as 20 years. The leisurely, friendly tour includes a stop in the kitchen for cookies and mint ice tea. For students and scholars, the library's extensive collection of Hawaiiana and plantation records is available by appointment.

Like other Hawaiian sugar plantations, Grove Farm was established at a significant point in the economic history of the islands. In the 1850's, the monarchy first began to sell land, and Hawaii entered the age of private property. Before this time, land was never sold but given in trust to subjects in pie shaped slices from the interior mountains to the sea, so that each landhold would include precious fresh water as well as coastline.

The Wilcox family, particularly two Wilcox women, made significant contributions to the development of Kauai. Elsie Wilcox, a Kauai School Commissioner, was the first woman in the territory to be elected to the Senate, and Mabel Wilcox, a public health nurse, was decorated by both France and Belgium for outstanding service during World War I. Elsie and Mabel restored **Waioli Mission House** in Hanalei (open T, Th, and Sat 9 am-3 pm), and Mabel planned the Grove Farm Homestead in 1971 when she was 89. Grove Farm Tours are conducted Monday, Wednesday, and Thursday at 10 am and 1 pm. Call for reservations (808) 245-3202 or write well in advance (PO Box 1631, Lihue HI 96766). Admission.

If the Grove Farm tour doesn't fit into your schedule, you can visit the **Kauai Museum** on Rice St. in downtown Lihue Monday-Friday 9:30 am to 4:30 pm. The Rice Building exhibits the "Story of Kauai"—the volcanic eruptions which shaped the land, the Polynesians who voyaged to the island in canoes, the missionaries who altered its culture, and the sugar planters who, like George Wilcox, defined much of its agricultural destiny. To complement this permanent display, the monthly exhibits in the adjacent Wilcox building feature the work of local artists as well as the contributions of Kauai's different ethnic cultures. For example, one summer we saw an exhibit of Japanese, Chinese, Hawaiian, and Filipino wedding dress and traditions. Another time, we explored a marvelous retrospective on Filipinos in Kauai, from their arrival in 1906 as poorly paid laborers to present day achievements in education and social work. The Folk Arts Exhibition includes quilt and *tapa* making, *lei* making, and Hawaiian games and sports. An exhibition on environmental challenges, 'Island Endangered Species,' explores issues of the 1990's. The museum shop has an extensive collection of books and maps on Kauai and Hawaii. Admission $3/adults (If you don't finish touring by the end of the day, you can get a free pass for the next!). For information about exhibits and lectures: 245-6931.

Halfway between Kapa'a and Princeville, be sure to visit the **Kilauea Lighthouse**, built in 1913, which once warned mariners away from Kauai's rugged north coast until technology replaced light flashes with radio transmissions. Come for spectacular views of the coastline and Mukuaeae island, and if you're lucky, a glimpse of Spinner Dolphins or Humpback Whales on summer vacation in the waves. This is the northernmost point of Kauai, and changes in weather are often first detected by the weather station here. Best of all, you will see a tiny part of the **Hawaiian Island National Wildlife Refuge**, which shelters more than 10 million seabirds in a chain of islands scattered over 1200 miles of ocean–like the Red-footed Booby. You will hear the amazing story of how seamen carried 4 tons of French prisms up a sheer cliff to build the giant clam shaped light. Open 10 am until 4 pm ($2 admission). Closed weekends, federal holidays. Hiking tour of Crater Hill on Tues., Wed, and Thurs at 10 am and 4 pm (1.5 hrs). Advance reservations necessary 828-1520.

The Hawaiian Art Museum and Bookstore at 2488 Kolo Road in Kilauea displays crafts by local artists, artifacts, and a large selection of Hawaiiana books and maps. Take home a free catalog.

More of Kauai's rare birds and plants can be seen at the **Koke'e Natural History Museum** in Koke'e State Park. If you are interested in exploring the island's natural history, visit the museum daily between 10 am and 4 pm (335-9975). Donations welcome!

The guided tour of **National Tropical Botanical Garden** in Lawai is an extraordinary opportunity to explore a 186 acre preserve of tropical fruits, spices, trees, rare plants, and flowers of astonishing variety and beauty. You can find 50 different kinds of banana and 500 species of palm. Instead of a formal garden, the plant collections are part of the natural landscape of the Lawai Valley. The tour includes a portion of the famed Lawai Kai, the Allerton family's spectacular private gardens, which have transformed this lovely valley into a rustic paradise, watered by an ingenious system of fountains, streams, waterways, and rocky pools. Among the shaded pathways, you will come upon a pavilion just perfect for relaxed contemplation, or a marble bench placed under a spreading, giant tree, or a statue reflecting a graceful image in a pool speckled with fallen leaves. As part of its research mission, NTBG trains botanists and preserves endangered tropical plants selected from all over the world. Reserve your tour well in advance by calling (808) 332-7631 or writing to PO Box 340, Lawai HI 96765, as the 2.5-hour tour, conducted 9 am and 1 pm daily, is usually fully booked and limited to the capacity of a 12-passenger van. The tour costs $15/pp and involves a two-mile walk. (A family membership ($25) includes free tours). If some of your party do not share a horticultural interest, you might plan to drop them off at Poipu Beach Park while you visit with the flowers!

If you'd like to explore the unspoiled forests of Moloka'i, you might consider taking the short flight to this island for the tour conducted on the second Saturday of each month by the Nature Conservancy of Hawaii. The 2,274 acre Kamakou Preserve contains rare birds and 250 kinds of plants, almost all of which live nowhere else except Hawaii, as well as spectacular gorges, rain forests, bogs and sand dunes. The all-day tour costs $5 for members of the conservancy and $10 for non-members. Contact the **Nature Conservancy of Hawaii**, 1116 Smith St., Suite 201, Honolulu HI 96817 (808) 537-4508. Reserve at least a month in advance.

Hiking and Camping

For those who have honed their bodies into the toughness of steel, hiking can be a spectacular way to see Kauai, for more than half of the island's 551,000 square miles is forestland, and many of its most beautiful regions are inaccessible by car. However, hiking Kauai is not without risks. Many trails can become dangerous from washouts and mudslides, and in the Na Pali coastal region, where trails are often etched into the sides of sheer cliffs, hikers must be wary of waves crashing over the rocks without warning, as well as vegetation which masks the edge of a sheer drop. A good friend, for example, broke his ankle last summer when plants gave way under his feet near the edge of a ravine.

Careful planning is a must. Before your trip, write the **Division of Forestry**, Kauai District, PO Box 1671, Lihue HI 96766 for a free information packet with maps and descriptions of trails in the forest preserves. For a similar free packet on the Na Pali region, write to the **Division of State Parks** at the same address. Bob Smith's wonderful **Hiking Kauai** describes a variety of hikes (PO Box 869, Huntington Beach CA 92648; $10.95). A large selection of books and maps for hiking and camping on Kauai and other Hawaiian islands is available from **Hawaii Geographic Society**, PO Box 1698, Honolulu HI 96806.

When you arrive on Kauai, call the **Division of Forestry** in Lihue (808/241-3433) for a report on current trail conditions. You can also call the **Hawaii Visitor's Bureau** in Lihue (808/245-3971) for advice and help in arranging hiking trips, and finding local guides.

The most famous trail, the Kalala'u, is a strenuous as well as spectacular 11 mile hike through the Na Pali cliff region. If your body is reasonably sound, you will enjoy the first few miles. This subsection, the Hanakapi'ai trail, has breathtaking views of the coast. About 1/4 mile past Ke'e Beach is a magnificent view of the beach and the Ha'ena Reefs. Two miles of rigorous up and down hiking will bring you to Hanakapi'ai Beach, nestled like a brilliant jewel in a picturesque, terraced valley (Hiking beyond this point requires a Day-use permit from the Division of State Parks). Unfortunately, this beach has currents far too dangerous for swimming, and the riptides can be so powerful that last year one unwary hiker standing in the surf at knee level was caught up in a sudden, large wave, pulled out to sea and drowned. The Kalala'u trail begins where paved road ends on the north coast, at Ke'e Beach, the last dependable source of drinking water. Plan on carrying your own drinking water on your hike because the bacterium *leptospirosis* is found in many of Kauai's rivers and streams. Important items: shoes with lug soles instead of jogging shoes or flip flops, sunscreen, insect repellent, a hat, even a nylon poncho. The trail can be muddy, and it is not appropriate for young children. For information about trails and conditions in Na Pali, visit or call **Jungle Bob's** (826-6664) in Hanalei, or the Division of State Parks (241-3444).

The Koke'e forest region and Alakai swamp are beautiful in a different way. Within this 4,345 acre wilderness preserve are 45 miles of trails, from pleasant walks to rugged hikes, as well as fresh water fishing streams. From the **Koke'e Lodge**, day hikers can choose from three trails which explore the plateau and Waimea Canyon rim, ranging from the half-mile Black Pipe Trail to the 1 1/2 mile Canyon Trail along the north rim of Waimea Canyon, past upper Wa'ipo'o Falls to the Kumuwela Overlook. From this perch you can see the canyon's 3,600-foot depth and 10 mile stretch to the sea. For longer hikes, you can arrange for guides, as well as hunting and fishing licenses, at the Koke'e Lodge. The Lodge also serves meals and cocktails, and rents cabins (including stove, refrigerator, hot showers, cooking and eating utensils, linens, bedding, and even fireplaces) for only $35-$45/night (maximum stay of 5 nights during a 30 day period). For information and reservations, write **Koke'e Lodge**, Box 819, Waimea HI 96796. (808) 335-6061. Bring warm clothes for cold nights, and remember, on Kauai as elsewhere, to lock your gear in the trunk of your car before you head for the trails.

You don't have to travel far to escape the rush! Conveniently located just outside of Koloa, **Kahili Mountain Park** offers reasonably priced, rustic cabins ($38 for two) and even more rustic one room 'cabinettes' ($22 for 2). The setting is beautiful and serene, a meadow backed by mountains with a view of the sea, and you can't beat the prices; extra persons cost only $4 a night. Contact Kahili Mountain Park, Box 298, Koloa HI 96756; (808) 742-9921.

Near road's end on the north shore, **YMCA Camp Naue** in spectacular Haena offers beachfront camping in bunk houses (or your own tent). It's popular with local clubs and families, but individual tourists are also welcome for $10 each per night (children half price!). For information about rules and reservations, contact YMCA of Kauai, Box 1786, Lihue HI 96766; (808) 246-9090 or 742-1200.

Several state and county parks allow camping, for example Anahola, Ha'ena, Anini, Salt Pond, and Polihale Beach Parks. Camping is also permitted in specified areas of the Na Pali region and other wilderness preserves. For information, permits, and reservations, write the Department of Land and Natural Resources, **Division of State Parks**, P.O. Box 1671, Lihue, HI 96766 or call (808) 241-3444. For information about hiking in the Alakai Swamp, or hiking and camping in Waimea Canyon, contact the **Division of Forestry** at the same address. Call (808) 241-3433. For kayaking/hiking on Kauai, contact **Adventure Kayaking International**, P O Box 61609, Honolulu HI 96822. For organized hikes, contact **Hawaiian Outdoor Adventures**, PO Box 869, Huntington Beach, CA 92648, directed by Robert Smith (714) 960-0389.

Riding and Running

The guided trail rides in Hanalei are a unique way to explore Kauai's beautiful north shore. **Po'oku Ranch** offers an hour's ride ($25) across the ranch lands; their two-hour 'Hawaiian Country Ride' takes you back towards the mountains for views. Po'oku's three-hour ride ($70) includes a hike to a waterfall for a picnic lunch and swim (826-6777). Groups of 10-12 proceed at a walk so that inexperienced riders will have no difficulty with their means of transportation. Nearby **Princeville Ranch** offers trail rides back into the Hanalei foothills. Limited to 4 persons ($68/2 hour ride), the group is small enough for an introductory lesson and for a pace determined by riding skill (826-6649). The morning ride (9 am -11:30 am) avoids the heat of the day. Wear sunglasses, and perhaps a hat which won't blow off; once you're on board, it's hard to climb down and chase it!

Those who live to run can dream about competing in the **Pepsi Challenge** 10,000 meter run in August (P O Box 1889, Lihue HI 96766) or the **Garden Island Marathon** on Kauai's west-end over Labor Day weekend (P O Box 3156, Lihue HI 96766). For a free schedule of the more than 90 races, triathalons and fun-runs statewide, send a SASE to Dept. of Parks and Recreation, City and County of Honolulu, 650 King St., Honolulu HI 96813. Remember the sun! Extra fluids and sunscreen are a must!

Golf Courses

Princeville Makai, Hanalei (826-3580), designed by Robert Trent Jones, Jr., is a 27 hole, world-class championship course with 3 challenging nines: Lake, Woods, and Ocean, famous for spectacular views and the dramatic 141-yard seventh hole, where the ocean, foaming like a cauldron, separates tee and green. Ranked Hawaii's best by *Golf Digest* Magazine, the new 18 hole, 7309-yard Prince Course is set in 390 acres of rolling pastureland. Daily fees, including carts, are $60/resort guests and $85/non-guests.

Kiahuna Golf Course, Poipu (742-9595), designed by Robert Trent Jones, Jr. is an 18 hole, par 70, links-style course, predominantly flat, with smooth, fast greens and tradewind challenges. At 6,353 yards from the tips, this course is geared more for the recreational golfer. Daily fees: $45/18 holes or $22/9 holes, including shared cart. $25 after 3 pm.

Poipu Bay Resort Golf Course, Poipu (742-1234), designed by Robert Trent Jones, Jr. is a par 72 Scottish links-style course, 6845 yards from the blue tees, along the ocean, adjacent to the Hyatt Regency. With cart, $85/guests ($115/non-guests).

Wailua Municipal Golf Course, Wailua (245-8092). Ranked in top 25 U.S. municipal courses by *Golf Digest*, this popular 18 hole, 6658 yard, par 72 course is built along the Pacific on rolling terrain amid ironwood trees and coconut palms. Fairways are narrow, greens smallish, and grass on the tough side. Fees are unbeatable: $11 on weekends or $10 on weekdays. Carts cost $11.50/18 holes or $6.75/9 holes, and pullcarts are available.

Kukuiolono Golf Course, Kalaheo (322-9151). 9 holes, par 35 with spectacular views. Honor system: $5/green fees and $5/cart.

Westin Kauai, Lihue (246-5078). Designed by Jack Nicklaus, the 262 acre Kiele course is designed for golfers with a 20-handicap or better. The front nine is long and rugged with many mounds and swales. The back nine runs out to the ocean, with spectacular views of waves crashing against the rocks, and prevailing tradewinds of up to 15 m.p.h. on the southeast corner. Restricted to 120 golfers a day with tee times at 15-minute intervals, it is an extra-long course (7000 yards) with 4 tees. The Kauai Lagoons course, ranked by *Golf Magazine* in "the top ten of America's most playable courses," is a shotmaker's course with many bunkers and more undulating greens. 6,942 yards from the tips. Fees are $95/resort guests and $125/non-guests.

Hawaiian Entertainment

Hawaiian entertainment is available in different settings at a range of prices. The most expensive is the combination show and Polynesian luau, a buffet including *kalua* pig, sweet and sour chicken, fish, fruits, *poi*, salads, and the like. On different nights of the week you can try this version at the Sheraton hotels or the Hyatt Regency in Poipu and Kapa'a, the Coco Palms Hotel or Paradise Pacifica in Wailua, or you can take an evening *luau* cruise with Smith's Boat tours. The Aston Kauai Resort features 'Leilani's *keikis*', gifted local children.

Some of the best shows are free! Monday, Wednesday, Friday and Saturday at 4:30 pm, come to the Coconut Plantation Marketplace south of Kapa'a for an excellent production! Or try the Kiahuna Shopping Center on Thursdays. Mosey over to the Coco Palms Hotel grounds and watch the dinner show, which starts around 9 pm, from the lawn. The shows vary nightly. At the Westin Kauai, a historic torch-lighting ceremony starts at dusk, complete with a procession along the beach as the Hawaiian paddlers come ashore and light the torches. The Coco Palms hotel in Wailua offers a similar free show nightly. The Waioli Hui'ia Church Choir performs hymns plus traditional Hawaiian dances and songs on Sunday nights at Bali Hai Restaurant, Hanalei Bay Resort. Come for dinner or listen from the lounge.

If you visit during summer months, you'll be able to enjoy another kind of festive entertainment, the *bon* dances held at island Buddhist temples to celebrate the ancestors of the congregation. Old and young dance together in large circles under colorful, lighted lanterns. Food, from shave ice to sushi, is usually available. At the last dance of the summer, the lanterns are set in rafts and towed out to sea near Spouting Horn. For a schedule of the dances, write to Waimea Shingon Mission, 3770A Pule Rd, Waimea HI 96796.

Island Tastes

For a taste of Kauai's local flavor, visit the Sunshine Farmer's Markets on Wednesdays in Kapa'a at 3 pm; on Mondays at noon in Koloa next to the firehouse; on Fridays at 3 pm in Lihue's Vidhina stadium, on Saturdays at 10 am at Waldorf School in Kilauea, and at 4 pm Thursdays in Hanapepe's First United Church of Christ. Come early for the best selection! From truck beds, tiny stands, or the trunks of cars, local farmers will sell their fruits, vegetables, and flowers at prices more reasonable than the supermarkets. And the manoa lettuce, as low as $1.00 for a half dozen small heads, will be fresh from the garden and taste of Kauai's sunny skies and salt air. You'll never want iceberg again! You may find avocados at 3 for $1; fresh basil, oregano, marjoram, or chives; a shiny dark purple eggplant with just the right sound when you thump it. You'll see bananas of all kinds—Williams, and Bluefield, and Kauai's special apple-bananas. Don't be put off by the short, fat, drab-skinned exterior, for inside is fruit the color of golden sand at sunset and a taste like bananas laced with apples!

If you see Iris at the Kapa'a market, she may offer you a slice of her star fruit to sample, or a selection of honey sweet orange with deceptively green skin, or a slice of juicy pineapple topped with passion fruit (or call her at 822-3568). The papayas will be giants, the Sunrise variety if you're lucky, for their red-orange center rivals the color of the sun. Try fresh limes to spark the papaya's mellow sweet flavor with tartness. Even if you aren't cooking, you'll be tempted by stringbeans as long as shoelaces, squash with squeaky skins, tomatoes still warm and fragrant, and all kinds of oriental vegetables with odd shapes. You may even find *leis* of pakalana or plumeria for $1 a strand! Be ready to bargain if you are buying in quantity from one seller, and take their advice about venturing into new tastes. On Wednesdays the market will be in the parking lot opposite the armory in Kapa'a. Take Kukui Road off Rt 56 and turn right at the end; then make the next right onto Kahau Road and look for the armory parking lot on your left. Many more people are coming to Kapa'a market, and you'll find a rope tied across the parking lot which looks—and serves—as a starting line, complete with a shrill whistle, to ensure an equal chance for buyers and sellers. It drops at five minutes to 3 pm, so don't be late! Most sellers price in $1 packages, so bring plenty of singles!

    For wonderful local fruits, stop at **Banana Joe's** just north of Kilauea on Rt 56. Joe makes one of the most scrumptious snacks known to man—a 'frostie' of fresh papaya, banana, or pineapple, created by freezing the fruits and then whipping them until they are light as sea foam. Maximum taste for minimum calories! Cocount shakes are delicious, too. Try Joe's pineapples, coconuts, and fresh red 'Cuban' bananas. At Joe's you'll also find several locally produced specialties. *'Anahola Granola'* (Try it with apple bananas) makes the perfect breakfast. *'Thai Vinegar'* (blended in Kilauea by 'The Secret Ingredient') is spectacular with fresh tomatoes! Also in Kilauea, on the road to the lighthouse, the **Martin Farm** roadside stand sells papayas on the honor system. You choose your fruits and leave your money in a box! (Closed Sundays). Sometimes, he makes fresh fruit smoothies! Just south of Kilauea on Rt 56, **Guava Kai Plantation** offers free guava juice and tours, 9 am to 9 pm daily near the mile 28 marker on Rt 56.

Though most fresh meats are flown into Kauai from the mainland, try beef raised on Kauai's sloping pastures. Some island farms raise tastier beef than others, so you have to know where to go. At the **N. Yoniji Store** on the Corner of Rice St. and Kalena St. in Lihue, you can find beef raised on the Rice Ranch in Kipu near Koloa, where Mrs. Rice still puts in a full day on horseback at 80. But then she's always been extraordinary. Plucked from her home on Kalapaki Beach by the *tsunami* of 1946, she just held tight to her infant son's nightgown and kept his head above water till help arrived! At Yoniji's store, you can glimpse Kauai before shopping centers! Browse through its remarkable assortment of furniture, clothing, and all kinds of foods!

To meet the growing demand from hotels and restaurants for superb fresh pasta, Tony, Gerry, and Rosario Iaskolk opened a state-of-the-art pasta factory, **Pasta D'Oro**. If they're not too busy, they'll show you around (245-8811). Look in the stores for their pasta with the black and gold label.

For the freshest local fish, try **Fish Express** at 3343 Kuhio Hwy (Rt. 56) just north of Lihue for filets of whatever has just been hooked—*shibiko* (baby yellow fin tuna), *ono, ulua,* and snappers of all hues—pink, grey, red. Prices vary with the weather, the season, even the moon, and are generally higher in winter, when fishing boats face rougher seas. The adventurous can try *opihi* (limpets) raw in the shell with seaweed, or smoked marlin. Your fresh fish selections can be vacuum sealed for shipping (245-9918). In Kapa'a, stop in at the inexpensive **Kuhio Market** on Rt 56, one block south of the park, or the higher-end **Pono Fish Market** on Rt 56 in Waipouli. The people are friendly and won't let you buy more than you need.

Shave Ice is an island favorite. Be sure to stop in at the **Wishing Well** in Hanalei for some of the best flavors and textures.

Kauai Specialties

For something truly special, visit Angeline Locey in Anahola for an unforgettable, authentic Hawaiian *lomi lomi* massage. Angeline is a *kahuna*, an 'elder' with especially gifted and gentle hands. The massage, which takes place in a special steam room of her own design, begins with a salt scrub with sea salt to clean your skin in preparation for the indescribable *lomi lomi*, fragrant with oil of coconut and lavender. Angeline and her assistant Anne call this place Muʻolaulani, and consider it sacred to the Hawaiian tradition of healing. This extraordinary, wonderfully relaxing two-hour experience costs a reasonable $75. Since the steamer may be shared by others, be sure to specify if you prefer being with your own sex. Call 822-3235 for reservations.

Something special to take home would be a batik design by Doris Foster. Her spectacular fabrics, printed and dried in sunny Spouting Horn, can be custom stitched during your stay into a reasonably priced Aloha shirt or sundress that you will see nowhere else. You can choose from many motifs, including sand dollars, sea shells, or tropical flowers, and from brilliant colors like turquoise, royal blue, cerise, and emerald, as well as more muted shades. You can see some of her fabrics at the Kapaia Stitchery or arrange a private appointment (742-1720).

Another talented batik artist named Trish designs wonderful cotton knit shirts with tropical fish in all the colors of sunsets over the ocean — wonderful pinks and oranges, purples and blues, yellows and reds. Trish works with the finest, softest, lightest cotton knit fabrics that feel like a whisper next to your skin. You'll never want to wear anything else again! The best selection of Trish's shirts is at the Wyland Collection at Kauai Village in Wailua, or order direct by mail from Designs by Trish, 319 Eggerking Rd, Kapaʻa, HI 96746.

Displayed in most island galleries, pottery by Mark White and Nancy Smith of Koloa is another special, unique souvenir. Their lovely bowls, platters, and cups are glazed to capture the beautiful colors and contours of Kauai's mountains, sea, and sky. As you sip your morning coffee back home, holding one of their generous, perfectly balanced mugs in your hand, you can close your eyes and imagine the island, waiting for you, sparkling in the sun.

Macadamia nut cookies taste like Kauai even if you're back home. Try several island bakeries: **Kauai Kookie Kompany**, sold in Big Save Markets or **Tip Top Bakery** in Lihue. In the Waipouli

Complex, **Po Po**'s mixes these heavenly nuts with chocolate chips or coconut into a confection Mrs. Fields would envy! **Kauai Soap** is especially gentle and fragrant because of painstaking care and high quality standards in its production. Try coconut or plumeria!

Kukui jams and syrups are the best! Be sure to sample some heavy, coconut syrup on your pancakes and guava-strawberry jam on your PBJs. Stop in at the factory in Kalaheo and make up your own gift boxes (four 6 oz jars cost about $6). You can pack them in your suitcases, or have them shipped (postage about $3/box). Call the office (332-9333) to be sure it's open. Take Rt 50 west, pass the junction with Rt 530, drive .8 mile and turn into a driveway on your right. There's no sign to mark the driveway, but you'll soon see the light blue building ahead. Don't pass up the Kukui specialty: macadamia nuts dusted with powdered chocolate!

If you're considering a wedding on Kauai, Kathryn Lowry can save you time, effort, and worry about the arrangements, including such special touches as horse drawn carriages and flower showers. She and her husband avoid the commercial locations, and instead help you find exactly what you might be looking for—a ceremony in a private garden, on a secluded beach, or even on a yacht. They can also arrange for flowers, a photographer, and the appropriate minister. Contact **Wedding in Paradise**, PO Box 1008, Kalaheo HI 96741. (808) 332-7177, or ask the Division of State Parks for a list of possible wedding sites (PO Box 1671, Lihue HI 96766).

Flower Leis

The fragrance of *pikake* or white ginger; the cool, silky touch of petals; the delicate yet rich colors of orchids and plumeria—even in words, flower *leis* conjure up moonlit nights and ocean breezes. No vacation is complete without one, especially on your last night.

Many stores offer ready-made *leis* in a refrigerated case, but these strings of imported carnations cannot compare with a local *lei* which reflects the traditions of the island as well as the individual artistry of the *lei* maker. Order your *lei* a day in advance and pick it up on your way out to dinner!

At **Fujimoto's** in Lihue (245-8088), a family-owned florist carries on local traditions. The *Mauna Loa lei* ($15), is a wide woven band of small purple orchids; very handsome, it is often given to boys at graduation. Or try the slender strand of fragrant green *pakalana*

($3/strand of 100 flowers), or another one of our favorites, the *lei* of white ginger, a spectacular creation of white buds so fragrant that heads will turn as you walk by. The tightly threaded ginger blossoms look almost like white feathers. Or if the blossoms are in season, try a beautiful *Ilima lei* made of papery orange-colored blossoms, very rare and difficult to string.

    The **Coco Palms Florist** in Wailua will even deliver if you are in the local area. The small, white *stephanotis*, similar in shape to a lilac blossom and even more fragrant, can be threaded in single strands ($2.50) or in a thick round "triple" *lei* ($12) of 300 flowers, striking to look at though heavy to wear. *Pikake,* a tiny and delicate white flower, is the Hawaiian lei for weddings and has a wonderful, spicy scent ($4.50/strand).

    Plumeria *leis* are the most common. Usually white or yellow and sometimes pink or deep red, the large blossoms have a wonderful perfume. A plumeria *lei* will last only a day, but it is relatively inexpensive, especially if you buy from Albert Christian in Anahola, who picks 7,000 blossoms each morning from his 300 trees. Look for his roadside stand on the eastern side of Rt 56, just south of Anahola. A single strand is $3, and you can request red, yellow and pink blossoms if you call a day ahead (822-5691). If you turn off the main road, follow the signs to 3805 Makio, where Emily Kealoha usually has a supply of leis ready, of plumeria and other blossoms.

    Surprisingly, you will have no trouble wearing a *lei* through agricultural inspection and onto the plane home, though the flowers quickly turn brown in air conditioning. Many shops will package *leis* for your return trip, so that they remain fresh to cheer your first cup of morning coffee back home!

Shopping

    It's hard to believe, but the best buys in the standard tourist gifts can be found at Woolworth's and Long's Drugs in the **Kukui Grove Shopping Center** in Lihue. Some specialty shops on the island really are special, however, and we keep finding more. Be sure to stop at **The Kapaia Stitchery** just north of Lihue on Rt 56 (Don't take the bypass road, or you'll miss it!). Julie Yukimura has collected a tasteful array of women's clothes at very reasonable prices. Many items are handcrafted by island seamstresses who still make quilts and dresses with the same care their own grandmothers did.

Beautiful vests, shawls, and dresses are priced well below what work of this quality sells for on the mainland. One woman in her '80's designs and stitches patchwork quilts, one featuring Japanese doll figures in different costumes, a great gift for a new baby. Men's Aloha shirts made by Julie's seamstresses sell for less than mass produced shirts in many stores, or you can custom order one from Julie's selection of 100% cotton fabrics in Hawaiian designs.

   On the north shore in Kilauea, **Kong Lung** offers a striking collection of antiques, souvenirs, beautiful gourmet cookware and tableware, and Hawaiian style shirts and dresses, including a special section for children. The owners have faithfully restored the old plantation store building, constructed of lava rock, and filled it with marvelous giftware, including their own line of Hawaiian jewelry. Also in Kilauea, stop in at **Hawaiian Art Museum and Bookstore** for one of the most interesting collections of books and artifacts anywhere! In Hanalei, don't miss the **Ching Young Store** for a wonderful collection of jewelry, clothes, and Hawaiian artifacts. Stop in at **Ola's** for puzzles, glass, jewelry, wooden bowls, and baskets by island artists.

   On the eastern shore, the once sleepy town of Kapa'a has grown into a trendy shopping area. You'll still find old veterans like Joe's Barber Shop, with a barber pole, right next to **Hot Rocket** selling neon clothes. **Progressive Expressions** displays the latest in surfing gear. On the corner, **Sandra's Crafts and Baby Creations**, you'll find handmade baby clothes, quilts, bibs and puppets, all at very reasonable prices, and if you're lucky, Sandra's daughter will be there and offer to show you photos of the horse she rides in 4-H. **The Only Show in Town**, next to Kountry Kitchen, offers an eclectic collection of inexpensive and unusual souvenirs and antiques.

   On the south side, Hanapepe is the latest small Kauai town to develop a cluster of specialty shops. At **Rainbow Art Glass**, Jeanette McLaren creates imaginative stained glass, featuring brilliant tropical flowers and birds (355-5645). Jeanette's husband operates **McLaren Woodworks** next door, crafting elegant furniture from beautiful koa wood. The McLaren's will create special orders to ship to the mainland. Across the street, **Amber** displays a wide range of original clothing hand-dyed and hand-stitched in Hanapepe. **Kauai Fine Arts Gallery** offers a wonderful collection of antique maps and prints, with a particularly fine selection of nautical and Pacific themes. Next door, the **Hanapepe Bookstore & Expresso Bar** (335-5011) is a great place for a mid-afternoon pick-me-up on a rainy day. Across the street, **Say Hey Baseball Card Shop** has, according to our 15-year old collector, one of the best selections he's seen anywhere. Silent auction cards are numbered; you stick your hand in your hat and may, just may, come up with a winner! The shop features all the newest cards, and the people are friendly. For a snack, try **Longie's Crack Seed Store**, where you'll find close to one hundred jars of sweet and sour treats, like shredded mango or dried plum. Mikey's favorite is "Bitter Lemon."

Kauai is a great place to shop for jewelry. **The Goldsmith's Gallery** in the Kinipopo Shopping Village features original jewelry crafted of gold, silver, and precious gems by five artist-craftsmen. Eric Vogt and the other award-winning designers will also be happy to show you albums of photographs of their designs, or to devise something special just for you, like a gold charm in the shape of a petroglyph or one of those fish you saw on the reef while snorkeling. On Rt 56 in Kapa'a, **Jim Saylor** specializes in jewelry designs with precious stones. Lovely rings, necklaces, and bracelets are on display, although Jim will also be happy to create something unique according to your specifications.

For coral jewelry, try **Gem** and **Linda's Creations** in Lihue, and the shops in the **Coconut Plantation Marketplace**. Cheaper prices can be found at the daily outdoor flea market at **Spouting Horn** or at the **Hawaiian Trading Post** at the junction of Rt 50 and Rt 530 near Koloa. At **Remember Kauai** or **The Shell Factory** on Rt 56 near the Coconut Plantation Marketplace in Wailua, you can have shell jewelry designed. Bring shells you find yourself, or select from the wide variety on hand in the stores. In Hanapepe, **Robert's** features reproductions of Hawaiian heirloom jewelry.

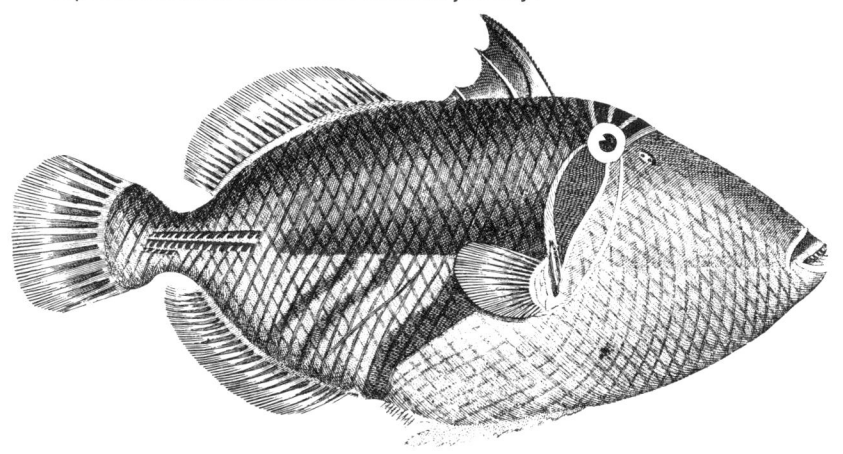

The island has many unique clothing shops. In Waipouli, stop in at **Marta's Boat** for children's wear, much of it handcrafted by Marta herself. In the nearby Kauai Village Shopping Center, **Wyland Collection** has an outstanding collection of hand-painted clothes. At **Nightengayles** in Kapa'a, you'll find an attractive assortment of colorful and comfortable women's clothes imported from all the islands, as well as interesting jewelry and artwork. **Bleu Papaya** displays original handpainted clothing designs.

A hard-working Kauai family has built the **Happy Kauaian Shops** from one store to more than a dozen branches in island hotels as well as the Coconut Plantation Marketplace. Their secret to success is reasonable prices for Hawaiian-style clothing and gifts, with a particularly good selection of children's clothes.

Kauai has several fine art galleries. In Koloa's **Kahana Ki'i Gallery**, one of the island's first galleries, you'll find a wide variety of work by Kauai's best artists— beautiful batiks, porcelains, jewelry, handpainted silk scarves, needlework, original oils, watercolors, and drawings, as well as Ron Kent's fine, almost translucent wood bowls (742-1408). **Stone's Gallery** in the Kukui Grove Center has a wide assortment of works by local artists (245-6653). At **The Gallery at the Waiohai** in Poipu, works by artists from all over the world with a common interest in Hawaii are displayed in beautifully crafted cabinets designed and created by Terry Wells of Kauai (742-9211). The blown glass and Ni'ihau shell *leis* are exquisite, and you'll also see pottery by Mark White and Nancy Smith. The restored plantation house at Kilohana houses several galleries, including **The Gallery** which features photographs, acrylics, prints, woodwork and other crafts by artists from Oahu and Kauai at a wide range of prices (245-9352), and the **Stones of Kilohana,** where you'll find artifacts of the Pacific, including ceremonial items, baskets, and koa bowls. **Kahn Galleries** at the Coconut Plantation Marketplace and Anchor Cove features paintings as well as fine Ni'ihau shell *leis* (822-5281). In the Princeville Center, **Montage Galleries** presents original art by Kauai artists.

A favorite with our children, **Wyland Galleries** have friendly staff and a fascinating collection of marine life paintings, particularly at the Anchor Cove branch. In the Kauai Village gallery, kids are fascinated with the tropical fish, and a spotted eel, in the 2,300 gallon aquarium.

In Poipu's Kiahuna Shopping Village, **Elephant Walk** displays elegant koa furniture and frames, as well as lovely prints and ceramics. Nearby, **Tideline Gallery** and **The Ship Store Gallery** often feature exclusive showings of works by artists of national reputation (742-7123). Look in at **Ralston Gallery of Fine Art** for fine watercolors, prints, and paintings (742-9755).

For the best buys in souvenir items, don't overlook department stores like Sears, Penney's, Longs, and Woolworth's at Kukui Grove Center. The **Whalers General Store** in Kiahuna Shopping Center and Coconut Plantation Marketplace often advertises specials on taste treats like macadamia nuts and coffee. If you're looking for the perfect T-shirt, try **Crazy Shirts**, whose shirts resist fading and shrinking. Wash them inside out. One of our favorite family stops is **M. Miura Store** in Kapa'a, an old-time local business where you can pick out souvenir T-shirts from a huge assortment at affordable prices, plus shorts, beachwear, *mu mus* and *aloha* shirts, and even boogie boards! Service is very friendly and the store uncrowded. If you need help with your camera, **Don's Camera Center** on Rice St. in Lihue can give you quick, efficient, professional advice. You can also rent cameras and have your film developed quickly.

Remember: Now that Kauai has entered the modern world, the Seven/Eleven accepts Visa and Master Card, and Foodland is open 24 hours!

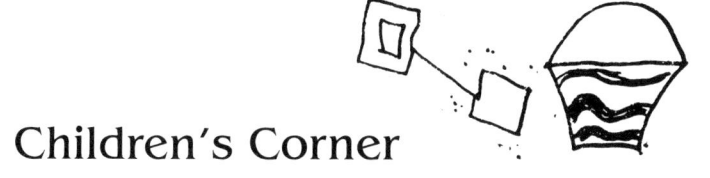

Children's Corner

The free hula show on Monday, Wednesday, Friday, and Saturday afternoons at 4:30 pm at the Coconut Plantation Marketplace in Kapa'a is a favorite with our children year after year. The show is great, with lots of music and dancing, and the kids don't have to sit in one place but can walk or run around and even climb some of the structures made from sugar mill machinery. While the kids enjoy the show, adults can browse the many shops.

Several beaches offer playground areas for children (Hanama'ulu, Poipu Beach Park), one offers lifeguard protection (Poipu Beach Park), and a few offer protected swimming areas for small children (Poipu Beach Park, Lydgate State Park). Fishing with nets is fun at the rivers behind the beaches at Anahola and Moloa'a, and at the tidal pools at Salt Pond Beach Park and Poipu Beach Park. If you bring some stale bread, the fish will swim right up to you. With this bait, kids can have lots of fun snorkeling even in very shallow water. The best spot for family snorkeling is Lydgate Park, where fish are trapped in the lava-ringed pools. For all around family fun in summertime, when the surf on the northern shore is gentle enough, our favorite beach is at Kalihiwai Bay, where you can wade and fish in the river, boogie board in the waves, and build sand-castles. In winter time, try Lydgate Park, or on the south shore, Salt Pond Beach Park and Poipu Beach Park. At any time, should you spot any small blue jellyfish on the sand, go to another beach for the day; these Portuguese men 'o war, which sometimes wash ashore after a storm, really sting!

Torchlighting ceremonies are fun for kids. Each evening at 7:30 at the Coco Palms Hotel in Wailua, torches in the grove are lit by Hawaiians in costume who recreate an ancient ceremony. Kids love the spectacle and don't seem to mind the black smoke! The Westin Kauai Hotel in Lihue also offers a free torch-lighting extravaganza.

The Westin is a children's wonderland. Kids will love a visit to the stable where Fergie, all of 19 hands high, loves a pat, and they will also enjoy a carriage ride through the hotel grounds. Throughout the hotel, the staff is pleasant and particularly accommodating to children, who will love the enormous pool, complete with bridge to the island in the center, and the five jaccuzzis. The hotel will take a whole morning to explore! Take the boat ride (It's free) across the huge lagoon. You'll pass by monkeys and birds and stop at Fashion Landing, where you can sample a shave ice at Sharkey's ($1) and browse the shops before the boat ride back.

If children collect shells and sand during visits to the beach, they can have fun with art projects on rainy days back home. Sand can be sprinkled over glue in all sorts of designs for "sand paintings." Kids will also enjoy gluing small shells to small plastic or cardboard boxes to give as gifts. Small shells can be glued onto pieces of driftwood or larger shells, or even made into necklaces.

With a plastic pail and an inexpensive net ($4 for an 8" net at Big Save), children can have lots of fun trying to catch fish trapped in tidal pools. Kids will also like to try Hawaiian treats, like Mikey's favorite, called 'Bitter Lemon' which he buys at the general store in Kealia.

Small tennis buffs can get some special practice with Meg Minton, who teaches tennis and swimming at the Sheraton Coconut Beach Hotel. Tennis and Swim Summer Camp meets 2 mornings a week for 3 week sessions (the first session begins in early June). Your child may register for single days, if there is space, or for private lessons. Call Meg at 822-3455, or write in advance (PO Box 830, Kapa'a HI 96746). To our kids, Meg is a favorite teacher, and tennis camp is "Ex!" During summer months and at Christmas, special daytime camp activities are offered for children of guests at the Westin, Waiohai, Hyatt Regency, and Sheraton Poipu Beach Hotels.

Kauai's public library system is very friendly. You can join local families for free puppet shows and talks, and even apply for a library card. For rainy days, rent a VCR and some movies. Cheapest rate is at Foodland ($2.99 for first tape; $1.49 for second) and selection of kidvid is pretty good. The new Blockbuster Video in the Safeway Shopping Center in Wailua is great!

Kids will love the Wishing Well in Hanalei, with the smoothest shave ice and lots of flavors (including root beer!) to choose from.

Special Mornings with Daddy

During our summer vacations, each of our four children plans a "Special Morning with Daddy," a wonderfully private adventure including dining, shopping, beaching and swimming. When they were small, they chose the same destination— the old Kauai Surf Hotel, which had ducks and a fish pond and a wonderful meandering swimming pool. Then the Surf closed. And while the new Westin was being built in its place, the children were growing older and beginning to look for wider horizons beckoning different interests. At first, this independence was risky business: what if one child could claim to have had a morning more special than anyone else's? Now they enjoy leading Daddy in different directions, exploring new, more exciting terrain.

At 15, Jeremy carefully plans his surfing adventure, which begins with breakfast at Kountry Kitchen in Kapa'a, where he can feast on 'Cheesy Eggs'– poached eggs with bacon on toasted english muffins, topped with lots of melted cheese sauce. There's a nod to tradition here: he's loved this dish since he was 4! After breakfast, it's off to the M. Muira store in Kapa'a, Jeremy's favorite shopping spot for the raddest shorts and shirts. Afterwards, he and Daddy head for Kealia Beach, where, if the tide is right, the wonderful, long rollers give spectacular boogie board rides. Daddy sits on the beach in his chair and reads his book, keeping a wary eye on the horizon for the big waves, as Jeremy glides along the glistening crest with the local kids.

Lauren still prefers to head south to Poipu. That's fortunate, for Daddy has always liked breakfast at the Waiohai Hotel, where the generous buffet at the Terrace Restaurant has a remarkably reasonable price ($13.50/adults; $6/kids). He loves the view of the ocean sparkling in the sun, and enjoys seeing the friendly waitresses who recognize him year after year no matter which short person ("Look how big you are!") he has in tow. After breakfast, it's off to his favorite beach, Poipu Beach Park, which nine-year-old Lauren also likes best of all. Thank heavens she still knows how wonderful it is to jump the waves with Daddy! At 12, Mikey prefers the breakfast buffet at the spectacular new Princeville Hotel, and then he and Daddy head for the surf at Hanalei Bay, where they can enjoy a catch and a long walk around the bay afterwards.

Mirah, at 17, prefers brunch, which begins at a more reasonable hour. She chooses Prince Bill's at the Westin, where after eating, she and Daddy board the hotel launch to cross the lagoon to Fashion Landing, where she browses in the shops, lingering longest at the store where you can sample all the perfumes and cosmetics and watch a video about skin care—in Japanese. After a shave ice at Sharkey's, and a brief rest for Daddy, they launch back to the hotel and head for the beach and pool. She still remembers the pool at the old Kauai Surf, almost on the same site, where she learned to swim under a wonderful waterfall which showered cold water on her hair.

Special Mornings With Daddy. When we first conceived the idea, we thought of how important they would be for each child. Now we're wiser– we know who the mornings are *really* for!

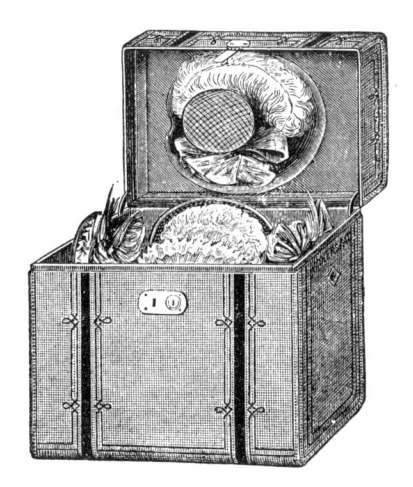

Travel Tips

If you are traveling with babies or toddlers, be sure to request "extra leg-room" seating well in advance of your trip—at the time you make your reservations or, at the very latest, two weeks before departure, and double-check to be sure your seat assignments are in the airline's computer before you leave. Getting your boarding passes in advance has another, very important advantage: your seats have priority if the flight is overbooked. Don't forget to enroll in the airline's "Frequent Flyer Plan." Bonus awards include free tickets, and even if it takes years for you to accumulate the required mileage, patience and persistence just might pay off! Enroll the children too! Be sure to bring along your child's car seat, which goes into the baggage compartment with your luggage, as Hawaii state law requires them for children under three.

Airline regulations require a minimum 70 minute layover in Honolulu to allow passengers and baggage to be transferred to inter-island connecting flights on Hawaiian or Aloha Airlines. However, there is a way to beat the system and minimize time wasted in the airport. After landing in Honolulu, proceed directly to the Aloha Airlines Terminal, a ten-minute walk or short bus ride. Check the departure schedule for an earlier flight, go to the ticket counter and see if you can get on, even as a stand-by if necessary (the computer data is often wrong, and stand-bys can usually get on). Changing your ticket from one carrier to the other can be done in a moment at the ticket counter. It used to be easy, when the terminals were side by side, to check schedules for both Hawaiian and Aloha Airlines at the same time, but airport renovation has separated them, and you must walk another ten minutes to check departures on Hawaiian Airlines. (Or let your fingers do the walking, and phone!) If you are able to change your flight, your luggage will remain on your originally scheduled flight, but you will be in Lihue with a head start, which you can use for filling out the forms on your rental car. Then you can drop someone off at the grocery store or leave the family at McDonald's while you go back for the baggage. On long travel days, especially with young children, this saved time can be a lifesaver!

Discount coupons can save you money! Entertainment Club (313- 637-8400) offers a terrific Hawaii coupon book for $30, including two-dinners-for-the-price-of-one offers at six Kauai restaurants and one companion-flies-free coupon on Aloha Airlines. Ask your travel agent about discount coupon books for inter-island flights on Aloha or Hawaiian. A party of six might be able to use them up on one trip!

Families who fly to Kauai from the east coast might consider staying overnight in California to help children make the difficult time adjustment in stages, particularly on the return home. After the long flight from Kauai to California, the kids can run around in the hotel, have some ice cream, and stay up as late as possible in order to push their body clocks ahead three hours while they sleep. If you can take a late morning flight out of California the next day, the kids can sleep late in the morning, and if you're lucky, they will wake up fresh for the second day's flight and be ready to adjust their body clocks another three hours. Traveling through two time zones is no snap, but this plan can make it a bit easier.

On that journey home, bad weather might delay your connecting flight from Lihue to Honolulu, and so you might consider taking a flight earlier in the day, before the inter-island flights get backed up. If you arrive in Honolulu so early that you can't hang around the airport, consider taking a cab to a Waikiki Beach hotel for brunch. The cab will cost about $25, but this plan is well worth it if you are traveling with young children, when the consequences of missing your flight to the mainland are too awful to consider! If you have more than five in your party, you can travel in luxury in a limo for no extra charge! Brunch at the Hilton Hawaiian Village, for example, can be fun!

To amuse little ones during the long flight, pack lots of small toys, crayons, dot-to-dot books, paper dolls and scissors and an "airplane present" that can only be unwrapped when the seatbelt sign goes off! Ask the cabin attendants for "kiddie packs" or cards right away as supplies are often limited. Pack a secret snack or toy for those awful moments when one child spills coke on another! Keep chewing gum handy to help children relieve the ear-clogging which can be so uncomfortable, even painful, during the last twenty minutes of the descent when cabin pressure changes. Sucking on a bottle will help a baby or toddler

To save shopping time, we bring as many beach and swimming toys as we can fit. "Swimmies" (arm floats) are great for small children to use in the pool. Small trucks for sand-dozing, frisbees, inflatable beach balls, and floats can be stuffed into suitcase corners! Boogie boards, by far the best swimming toy, are expensive, but can be brought home in the baggage compartment after your vacation (packed in a pillowcase!). We found the best prices at Gem in Lihue, the M. Miura store in Kapa'a, Wailua Surf Shop in Wailua, and Progressive Expressions in Koloa, which also handcrafts surfboards and skim boards. Boogie boards are better balanced than the cheaper imitations, and even small children enjoy trying to ride them. Caution: they can be hazardous in a pool; a small child who tips over in deep water can be trapped underneath.

When two suitcases disappeared during our flight home in 1982, we learned some lessons the hard way about packing. Now we pack a change of clothes, bathing suit, and toilet articles for each family member, as well as any prescription drugs, in a carry-on bag just in case someone's suitcase is lost temporarily. We also distribute everybody's belongings in every suitcase, so that no one person is left without clothes if a suitcase is lost permanently. And we label each bag clearly *inside* where the label can't be accidentally detached. Since one of our missing suitcases contained all our exposed film, a heartbreaking loss, we now use mailers and send each roll off as we finish it. Incredibly, lightning struck twice, and two more suitcases disappeared three years later. Replacement-cost property insurance on our Homeowner's insurance policy has certainly turned out to be a wise investment, for the airline's insurance limit is $1,250 per passenger, unless you purchase increased protection at the ticket counter before the flight (usually $1 per $100). Airlines typically subtract 10% of the purchase price for each year you have owned an item, exclude cameras and jewelry, and may take up to six months to process a claim.

If your luggage is missing or damaged, save all baggage-claim stubs, boarding passes, and tickets, and be sure to fill out an official claim form at the baggage supervisor's office *before* you leave the airport. Most clearly tagged luggage makes its way to the owner within 24 hours. If your luggage is orphaned for longer and you are out of town, most airlines offer emergency funds of $25 a day if you present receipts. Call daily for an update on your missing bags!

Tired of hotels? For information about private homes on Kauai that take paying guests, contact Bed and Breakfast Hawaii, PO Box 449, Kapa'a HI 96746 (808) 822-7771.

Traffic Hints

We never thought we'd write a section like *this*! However, you'd be wise to avoid the main road, Rt 56, between Lihue and Kapa'a between 4 and 6:30 pm on weekdays. Take the new 'bypass' road which takes you north from Lihue (near the airport) to just north of Hanama'ulu. You'll avoid the traffic on Rt 56, but not for long. You'll have to get onto Rt 56 at Hanama'ulu, and it may be stop all the way to the traffic light at Wailua, perhaps even to Kapa'a. Kauai is still rural as far as the infrastructure goes—just two-lanes, all around the island! Polish your left hand turn skills, try not to drive between 4 and 6:30, and be patient. Remember, you're on vacation!

While driving your rental car on Kauai, keep this in mind: speed limits are strictly enforced, especially in residential and business areas, and so is the seat belt law. It's illegal to make a U-turn in a "business district," even if it doesn't look like much of a business district. There's not much crime on this island, so you can guess how the police occupy their time!

Suggestions From Our Readers

The Patlers of Mill Valey, CA share their "special afternoon with Daddy" : walking the beach at Hanalei Bay, crossing over to the Waioli Mission grounds to swing and shoot baskets, and ending up at the Wishing Well for the best shave ice! Macadamia nut ice cream over shave ice is a favorite, as is *lillikoi*.

Polihale Beach on a very rainy day is not a good idea, according to the Franks of Edgewood, Kentucky. "We mired our car in the muddy cane road and were lucky to be pushed out by some plucky Wyoming tourists!" This advice is true of all Kauaian dirt roads.

The Dawsons of Los Angeles suggest a visit to the Waioli Mission House and Church in Hanalei. Sunday services are conducted in Hawaiian as well as in English, and the very friendly family atmosphere is evident in the announcement at the top of the Sunday Bulletin: "Our *keikis* are apt to wander during church. They do this because they feel at home in God's house. Please love them as we do." Call 826-6253 for information.

The McILheneys enjoyed a mountain bike ride down a trail beginning in Koke'e. 'Downhill Kauai' supplies equipment and arranges transportation.

Aleena Paras-Kopecky of Portola Valley loved the fruit smoothies made fresh at the Martin Farm on the road to Kilauea Lighthouse.

Susie Winston of Alexandria, Virginia suggests a stop at Jungle Bob's in the Ching Young Village Center in Hanalei prior to snorkeling on the north shore. "The people are so friendly and give very helpful advice. When I asked about anti-fog drops for my mask, the salesman gave me some of his own!"

About Secret Beach, Donna Madden of Orinda California writes "Either you kept a secret from us, or the beach kept its secret from you, because it is sometimes a nude beach...We were surprised when we got to the bottom of the path and ran into a man with long bond hair wearing nothing but a guitar." Each to his own music!

Restaurant Index

A
Al and Don's, 70
All Kine Burgers, 146

B
Bali Hai, 49
Banana Joe's, 171
Barbecue Inn, 71
The Beach House, 124
Beamreach, 51
Brennecke's Beach Broiler, 126
Brick Oven Pizza, 128
The Bull Shed, 72

C
Cafe Hanalei, 53
Cafe Portofino, 73
Cafe Zelo, 54
Camp House Grill, 129
Cantina Flamingo, 130
Casa di Amici, 55
Charo's, 56
Chuck's Steak House, 57
Club Jetty, 74

D
Dani's, 74
Hanalei Dolphin, 143
Dondero's, Hyatt Regency, 132
Dragon Inn, 75
Duke's Canoe Club, 76

E
The Eggbert's, 77
El Cafe, 99

F
Fast Foods, 122-23
Flamingo Cantina, 130
Foong Wong, 59

G
The Green Garden, 147
Gaylord's, 91

H
Hamura Saimin, 78
Hanalei Dolphin, 60
Hanalei Gourmet, 64, 123
Hanalei Shell House, 64
Hanama'ulu Restaurant &
  Tea House, 79
House of Seafood, 133
Hyatt Regency Hotel
  Dondero's, 132

I
Inn on the Cliffs, 81

J
JJ's Broiler, 86
Jacaranda, Kauai Hilton, 83
Jacques's Bakery, 26, 122
Jimmy's Grill, 84

K
Kalaheo Steak House, 150
Kapa'a Fish & Chowder, 87
Kauai Chop Suey, 88
Kauai Hilton Hotel
  Jacaranda, 83

Keoki's Paradise, 135
Kiibo, 89
Kilohana, 91
King and I, 90
Kintaro, 94
The Koloa Broiler, 137
Kountry Kitchen, 96
Kukui Nut Tree Inn, 96

L
La Cascata, 65

M
Makai, 97
Ma's Family, Inc, 98
Mustard's Last Stand, 124

N
Naniwa, 138
Norberto's El Cafe, 99

O
Olympic Cafe, 101
Ono Char Burger, 101, 123
Ono Family Restaurant, 102, 123

P
A Pacific Cafe, 103
Panda Garden, 105
Plantation Gardens, 139
The Planters, 106
Portofino Cafe, 73
Prince Bill's, 107
Princeville Hotel
  Cafe Hanalei, 53
  La Cascata, 65

S
The Seashell, 110
Sharky's Fishmarket, 111
Shell House, Hanalei, 64
Sheraton Coconut Beach
  Voyage Room, 117
The Sizzler, 113
Sumo Restaurant, 114

T
Tahiti Nui, 68
Tamarind, Waiohai Hotel, 141
Taqueria Nortenos, 142
Tempura Garden,
  Westin Kauai, 115
Tip Top Motel, 117
Toi's Thai Kitchen, 148
Tropical Taco, 123

V
The Voyage Room
  Sheraton Coconut Beach, 118

W
Wailua Marina, 119
Waiohai Hotel
  Waiohai Terrace, 143
  Sunday Brunch, 145
  Tamarind, 141
Waipouli Deli, 121
Westin Kauai
  Inn on the Cliffs, 82
  Prince Bill's, 107
  Tempura Garden, 114
Wishing Well, 172, 181
Wrangler's Restaurant, 151

Z
Zelo's Deli & Expresso Bar, 54

Index

A
Alakai Swamp, 166
Anahola Bay, 28
Anini Beach, 19

B
Banana Joe's, 171
Barking Sands, 42
baseball cards, 177
batik designs, 173
Beach Safety, 44-45
Bed and Breakfast, 185
boat tours, 158-61
Bon Dances, 170
boogie boards, 184
Brennecke's Beach, 37

C
children's corner, 179
children's parks, 179
Ching Young Store, 176
clothing, 175-79
cookies, 174

D
Division of Forestry, 166,167
Division of State Parks, 167
Donkey Beach, 29

F
farmer's markets, 171
Fast Foods, 123-24
fresh island fish, 172
fruit stands, 171
FAA Regulations, 154-55

G
galleries, 177
Garden Island Marathon, 168
golf, 168
Grove Farm Museum, 162

H
Ha'ena Beach Park, 14
Hanalei Bay, 18
Hanama'ulu Beach, 32
Hawaiian foods, 170
Hawaii Visitor's Bureau, 166
Hawaiian Island National Wildlife Refuge, 164
health foods, 170
helicopter tours, 154-158
hiking, 165-7
horseback riding, 168
hula shows, 169-70

I
Infinity Beach, 40
inter-island airlines, 183

K
Kahili Mountain Park, 167
Kalala'u Trail, 166
Kalapaki Beach, 33
Kalihiwai Bay, 20
Kapa'a Beaches, 31
Kapaia Stitchery, 175
Kauai Museum, 163
Kauai Village Center, 178
Ke'e Beach, 13
Kealia Beach, 30
Kekaha Beaches, 41
Kilauea Bay, 23
Kilauea Lighthouse, 164
Koke'e Lodge, 166

Koke'e State Park, 166
Kong Lung Store, 176
Kukui Grove Center, 175
Kukui Jams, 173
Kukuiolono Golf Course, 169

L
Larsen's Beach, 25
Lawai Kai, 164
leis, 174-5
leptospirosis, 45,166
libraries, 180
Lumahai Beach, 18
luggage/packing, 185
luau shows, 169-70
Lydgate State Park, 31

M
Mahaulepu Beach, 35
Major's Bay, 42
map, 16-17
Marine Weather, 45
Martin farm, 187, 172
men 'o war, 45
Moloa'a Bay, 27
Mt Waialeale, 157
museums, 162

N
Na Pali, 157, 160, 166
Na Pali Coast tours, 158-61
National Tropical Botanical Gdns, 164
Nature Conservancy,HI, 165
Ninini Beach, 34

P
Po'oku Ranch, 168

Poipu Beach Park, 37
Polihale Beach, 42
Princeville Makai golf, 168
Princeville Ranch, 168

R
running & jogging, 168

S
Salt Pond Beach Park, 39
Secret Beach, 21
Shipwreck Beach, 36
shopping, 175-78
Spouting Horn Market, 176
sunscreens, 121
Sunshine Markets, 170

T
T-shirts, 178
tennis camp, 180
traffic, 186
tropical fruits, 170
travel tips, 182-84
Tunnels Beach, 14

W
Wailua Municipal Golf, 169
Waimea Canyon, 166
weddings, 174
Westin Kiele Golf, 169

Y
YMCA camp Naue, 167

Z
zodiacs, 158-61

Order Form

Please send _____ copies of the
Kauai Underground Guide to:

I enclose $6.95 plus $2 shipping and handling.

Papaloa Press

362 Selby Lane
Atherton CA 94027